Creative Nonfiction

C. Dougla͟ Atkins, *Series Editor*

Naming the Light

Naming the Light

A WEEK OF YEARS

ROSEMARY DEEN

UNIVERSITY OF ILLINOIS PRESS : URBANA AND CHICAGO

© 1997 by the Board of Trustees of the University of Illinois
Manufactured in the United States of America
P   5   4   3   2   1

This book is printed on acid-free paper.

Library of Congress Cataloging-in-Publication Data
Deen, Rosemary.
Naming the light : a week of years / Rosemary Deen.
p.   cm. — (Creative nonfiction)
ISBN 0-252-06572-7 (pbk. : acid-free paper)
I. Title. II. Series. III. Series: Creative nonfiction (Urbana, Ill.)
AC8.D487   1997
081—dc20   96-4529
                                                      CIP

To Leonard Deen and Marie Ponsot

and in memory of Estelle and Harold Fowle

Then this immensive cup
  Of aromatic wine,
Catullus, I quaff up
  To that terse muse of thine.
—ROBERT HERRICK

Contents

Acknowledgments

"Cat's Cradle," "The Maze," and "Mulch" appeared in *Antioch Review* 51, no. 4 (Fall 1993): 596–604. © 1993 by the Antioch Review, Inc. Reprinted by permission of the editors. "The Need for Green" appeared in shortened form as "How Green . . ." in *Commonweal* 121, no. 12 (June 17, 1994): 31. "Denizens," "The Genius of the Place," "History," and "Raccoons" appeared in *Kenyon Review* n.s. 16, no. 2 (Spring 1994): 1–9. "First Fruits" and "Out and About" appeared in *Kenyon Review* n.s. 17, no. 22 (Spring 1995): 121–26. "Feasting and Preserving" appeared in *Kenyon Review* n.s. 18, no. 2 (Spring 1996): 76–78. "Elation," "Handy," "Orientation," and "Prolific and Devourer" appeared in *Raritan: A Quarterly Review* 14 (Fall 1994): 68–82. "Michaelmas" and "Theory of Descant" appeared in *Raritan: A Quarterly Review* 15 (Spring 1996): 111–18.

I must thank various readers of these "letters": Nanine Bilski-Dowling, who said the beginning word; my intimate readers, Leonard Deen, Marie Ponsot, Bette Weidman, Louise Smith, Sally Pleet; friends and acquaintances of unremitting intelligence whose readings showed me what discrimination is, David Kleinbard and Maureen Waters, Don McQuade, Marilyn Hacker, Phillip Lopate; and readers I've never met, like Robert Fogarty, Richard Poirier, and G. Douglas Atkins, who even at an unknown distance welcomed me. Finally thanks to Becky Standard, who minded every word and every point, to Ann Lowry, for her equable intelligence, and to both for their good work and goodwill.

Introduction : A Week of Years

These essays began when a friend said, "Why don't you write something like the things you tell me when we walk in your garden?" These would not be "how to" things, for if I spoke of the garden directly, it was often ruefully. In nature I sympathize with Darwin's complaint when his experiments went haywire: "all nature is perverse & will not do as I wish it." If it were about the garden, a piece of writing was bound to be mildly comic.

Writing essays—making them very small, making everything work twice, seeing gardens turn into metaphor—proved irresistible. When they got going, however, the essays wouldn't stick with the garden but let in whatever the words brought in: an old stone house, a medieval king, a fresco, a motet. So the essays are comic in the sense that they are prone to liberty. They leap; they don't care for the explicit. But I hope the gaps are synaptic, that the language, in the absence of narrative, makes the connections.

The essays divide themselves, it seems to me, into a week of "years." I mean "year" not as a fixed segment but as a kind of timing: ample time, time-enough. "Give me time-enough," we say. A garden always means leisure, even when it's stolen leisure. You can see right away that's imagined time: time for the outdoors to come indoors, for an idea to stretch toward its reversal, for days to equal nights again, for fair winds and following waves. These times, like tempi in music, suggest that timing is also mood or mode.

Here are some of the centers or stopping places in this "week." Year One is mostly about the need for green, for light that feels green in the body, and the way we try to name light as something bodily. That's where we begin, I suppose. And it's in the light of the body that animals come close.

Year Two is directional all ways, or you could say it's about edges: weeds at one edge, the wild at another, the sky, where we need to find an edge to find ourselves, the edge back of us in the past, and children who push the edge ahead.

Year Three is a span, roughly between the equinoxes, from the brink of irresistible energy to fading light and the man who doesn't recognize that because he works in his own light anyway.

Year Four curves down and up. It begins in late summer in plenty and feasting that brings us together with other feasters, but it descends toward the nadir where only a cat's cradle and mute consonants connect us, if they can. But we do connect; even eye-beams hold us together.

Year Five starts out with high summer and goes from high heroes to feet and hands. These essays are partly about how we try to keep on working with the voices from our lives talking all at once in our heads. I suppose that's why music keeps coming into the writing. Musicians have so many good theories of working with several voices, all singing differently and together.

Year Six is renaissance in some way or other. Year Seven is—but you get the idea. I leave you with Year Seven and a lens to read it. These are the gatherings I see now, but you'll read the years in your own ways.

One reader of the manuscript wanted to omit three of the essays on the grounds that they might daunt readers. That was a polite way of saying, I think, that they are bookish. But others thought you readers weren't so easily daunted. If an essay gets stiff, a reader can chuck it. There's another one coming along right away. Anyway, these essays didn't ask me before they strayed into books or even paintings. The raccoon got into *Paradise Lost* somehow, and the rainworm went further.

Words, like nature, seem to enjoy a will of their own, though that is not rue but happiness. The rainworm ended up in *The Republic*, but I couldn't help it. You remember the story we hear at the end of *The Republic* about the visit of a man named Er to the immortal world where souls are punished for their injustice or enjoy the heaven of justice till the time comes for them to choose a new life on earth. In the immortal world Er sees a wonderful model of the whole universe, spheres within spheres, in the shape of a spindle resting on the knees of Necessity.

I was writing, not thinking about any of this, but thinking in my notebook about how the weather begins at the equator and how the equatorial winds spin fastest of any on earth, like the rim of a wheel, as naturalists say. But also like the outer whorl of a spindle. Then I too saw the spindle resting on the knees of Necessity, and I knew where the rainworm came from. You can't name without words, so you might as well listen to them.

I'm afraid this is not a "dramatic" book. Someone remarked to me recently that my life has not been as chaotic as some. I think she meant my life as it appears in writing, but it's true that I have not been thrown out of orbit in the terrible way many people have experienced. Though I've often felt I was holding my life together by main force, my teeth rattling, that's no different from most people's lives, which (mercifully) are not big with tension and suspense. That's why we need genuine drama: to see with a present intensity what human action can be when an irreversibly present moment tests it. For this we need drama in big art forms, something more than media thrills, interesting though these are.

But on a day-to-day basis, I think, we need the language we speak to be alive in metaphor, the experience of words meaning what they say. Metaphor is stubborn or democratic or erotic, depending on how you look at the way its parts persist in a longing for union with a difference that will always keep them apart. There's something in impediment we must admit, even in lives that are ordinary rounds, beginning and stopping, like small essays.

Naming the Light

Year One

1 : *The Need for Green*

We need to sense green life. In winter when I come home late from my evening class and pass through the kitchen, I pause at the counter where I keep a collection of small plants under a long plant light. I set my book bag down and gaze at the button fern, refined and sturdy, the maidenhair uncoiling green curls from its satisfying, wiry black stem. The bird's nest fern is always rolling a shiny new leaf out of its bird's nest heart. In a homemade Wardian case the leaf of a fancy begonia sprouts tiny new plants from each cut in the leaf vein.

But it isn't wonders that keep me there; it's simply the sensation of green. I feel it in some somatic core, as you feel clear water quench a serious thirst. "What have you been doing in the kitchen for the past hour?" says Leonard Deen when I come into the living room. "An hour?" I'm surprised. "I was just looking at the plants."

Leisurely summer weeding gives the same pleasure of purely touching green. You go out in the early morning, in some morning-shaded spot, perhaps with your morning cup in hand. A few weeds have got a nice green start. You sit down at the border and pull them out, one by one: root—hairy and delicate, still clinging to the good soil—stem, and greeny leaves. The oriole keeps making his one assertion, which always breaks off in the middle. You're down in the green, tranquil and balanced. What you do will not be undone in the next twenty minutes. The weed green passes into your hands and into your soma.

The plants you have freed gain ground and their own greenness. They articulate themselves more, up there in the light; but you're enjoying the dumbness of the simple, the single green. You are one with the weeds, not with your plants now. It's a dialectical oneness, because you're sorting out and throwing away: "This is true; this is not true." But it's the dialectics of poise, not of struggle or heroism. You're not laboring at something to get it over with but acting on each part with the energizing patience of green.

I realize there are nongreen places in the great world, where sky and air are everything, or rock and height. And there are greener worlds than mine, which may be almost enough to satisfy the need for green. Once in the south of England during a June vacation of almost constant rain, Leonard and I found ourselves back of Winchester Cathedral looking at a sign that said "Water meadow walk to St. Cross. One mile." Until we saw the sign we hadn't known we wanted to go to St. Cross, whatever that was. The usual gentle rain was falling. We set out along a single-person path beside a small stream flowing clearly over light brown gravel through what was presumably the water meadow. The grass was over our heads. It was a world of never-ending grass; all the cattle of the sun couldn't have consumed it. There was no one about, and no other world than this.

The stream gradually grew a little bigger, supported a few water fowl and a few fish. Our feet wet on the path, our heads wet in the green watery air, it was hard to tell the one water from the other. The green of the water grasses seemed simply expressed into the green rain above them. Leonard realized this was the Itchen, whose stained-glass image we had just seen in Silkstede's chapel, Isaak Walton sitting pensively by the banks where we walked now. Occasionally we saw a house with its own small bridge over the stream and its own locked bridge gate—though the stream was hardly a barrier simply to stepping across. The houses appeared remote in the watery air, but in the garden of one I saw a woman with an umbrella picking lettuces. We crossed a modern road, which was by then unbelievable, and plunged once more into the world of the River Daughter. A handsome, very blue-eyed young woman in slicker and Wellington boots passed us and said we were on the right way.

St. Cross turned out to be a twelfth-century "hospital for poor brethren." Its attendant asked us whether we required bread and ale after our journey, as he was bound to give it to travelers who asked for it. "Do you really give it?" I asked. "Do you ask for it?" he replied. We hadn't the temerity to ask. We wandered through old rooms. There were a few tools and kitchen implements, but mostly the rooms were filled simply with Corot light, watery and clear. When we left, the attendant was gone, but I noticed a sign on the desk which said his name was Mr. Heaven. Then we went back through the green water meadow as we had come. In the train on the way back to London, as I got out the extra pair of dry socks I always carried in England, I felt it had been a satisfying day.

Green, as it happens, is my most unfavorite color. I mean the green one is offered in wall paint, rugs, sofas, and dress goods. It discomforts me. Leonard pretends to find this amusing as he sees me come in from one of my watering forays into the tomato plants growing higher than my head. "If green is your most unfavorite color, then why are there leaves growing in your hair?" he says, plucking them out and placing them greenly in my hand.

2 : *Summer Kate*

I'm going to give my neighbor a beautiful daylily that has increased in my garden. It's a tall plant crowded with light lemonish flowers, fragrant and slightly old-fashioned, a simple lily form, but less stiff and waxed than true lilies. The large clump blooms abundantly, and when I pass by the flowers in the morning they dapple in the birch light and waft lemon scents.

My neighbor, who is renting the charming Revolutionary War stone house down the road, is a French woman, beautiful, full of style, and has never gardened before. She begins by borrowing some gardening tools, an ancient and customary gesture, selecting a hand cultivator and a small spade she says is just her size, the "Lady's Garden Spade" its manufacturer rather unnecessarily calls it. She intends to weed and "plant flowers," an expression which reminds me of my childhood's first gardening effort. I had picked some flowers, probably from a neighbor's garden, and "planted" them all in a row. But they didn't respond to my borrowing. Since then I have sometimes done better and sometimes no better than that.

When she's finished, she and I survey the results. She's planted a couple of six packs of marigolds all in a row. They are tiny, almost leafless plants each with one small flower abloom on the top. But in a week or two they will bush out into abundant, pungent green leaves and flourish their blossoms in the western light, looking beautiful against the old stone of the house. Her beginner's ambition has carried her into another patch of weeding and clearing, and she wonders what to plant there. I take a look. It's a circle outlined by stones belling out from two dispirited peonies. I have just the thing for it, I say, if she doesn't mind a perennial. I'm not sure she knows this English word, but she gallantly says she doesn't mind perennials.

I fetch my hardy spade apologetically, but I suspect she's "weeded" by seizing and pulling off the tops of the tough, perennial weeds. When I've dug the circle good and deep, I return to my garden to heave out a great clump of daylilies and wheelbarrow it down to the stone house, its lancing leaves nodding in the dappled afternoon light of the road, balancing on its great root ball.

In place it looks a handsome fountain of green, though I'm rather embarrassed that it has no flowers yet, not even budded stalks. I explain that it will have many flowers later, in July, but think to myself that July must seem far off to an enthusiastic May gardener. "What is it?" she says, and I start to say it's Summer Kate.

But I don't know its real name, though I could call it "False Hyperion." My friend Molly Finn had kindly given me a plant from a clump given to her under the name Hyperion. I was glad to enter this circle of plant giving, though I already had a specimen, because Hyperion is an austere beauty, chary of bloom and proliferation. It's old, introduced in 1925, but its purity and the glamor of its name make it memorable—and overpriced for a fairly ordinary plant.

When Molly's plant bloomed, however, it was obviously something new. Its scapes were sturdy, not the slender wands of true Hyperion, and it loved the sun and set about blooming abundantly long before Hyperion, cool in the shade, had decided what allotment of buds it was going to give me this year. But the new plant was nameless until I realized that I could call it after a friend or admired acquaintance in the old tradition of naming favorite plants. But who? Well, there was my summer neighbor, Agnes.

And now I'm afraid you'll think this is a trifle complicated, though it's simple if you have patience with a narrative. One day my daughter Catherine said to Agnes that she didn't like her name and would prefer to be called Kate. I suppose she was about fourteen at the time. "What a coincidence!" said Agnes. "I've never liked my name either and would prefer to be called Kate." In fact, Agnes's husband, Charlie, didn't like his name either and would prefer to be called Reggie. Catherine and Agnes agreed to call each other Kate during the summer.

Summer agreements, though, are soft as summer winds. Somehow Agnes remained Agnes, and Catherine got older and decided that she was Catherine after all. But I regretted a little that a wish doesn't come true, especially a summer wish. So I gave Agnes a plant of my incognita to grow by her screen door, and we called it Summer Kate.

How could I say all this to my new, charming French neighbor? And why should I?—except that names are webs of meanings, are history and knowledge, even knowledge of falsehood. A Lady's Garden Spade will hardly spade at all except in ground well dug and turned by the spade we call a spade. And marigolds, those tough, rather ungraceful plants, are nevertheless "Mary's Gold," one of hundreds of "Mary" or "Lady" plants named so in Europe in the Middle Ages and later in the New World. We are all balanced on our roots. It was planted by women and men against stone walls older than those of our Revolution, in a sun younger than ours. And a *per*-ennial lives *through* the years, though its gardeners are annuals, as far as they know.

My new neighbor, as it turns out, calls herself Katy. But I thought I would just give her the plant, without any other warrant than its habit of catching the light and its own flourishing good faith. So I said, "It's a daylily, which is not a true lily, and its name is Summer Kate."

3 : *Mulch*

It's time to mulch the vegetables. The tomatoes—our favorite Belgian Giants, those fleshy pink beauties—are so well spaced that there's plenty of room for weeds to luxuriate among them. When I consider mulch, my thoughts turn to the Earl of Osterhoudt. Earle Osterhoudt is his name really, but he's so magnificent in his works and ways that his name ought to be a title. It does signify an old American tradition—there were probably Osterhoudts among the Huguenots who came to this county in the seventeenth century.

Mr. Osterhoudt shows that the stock has not diminished. He must be six foot three, weighs over two hundred and fifty pounds, and has a commanding presence and voice. The voice, in fact, booms out of that mighty chest and seems to rock me slightly so that I step back, the better to sustain the whole effect. But Mr. Osterhoudt wishes to keep his listener within range and advances as I retreat till I'm well placed with my back against the rail fence of his pasture. So much physical presence with all its implicit psychic energy has a tremendous aura—it's not simply the voice one needs to stand back from. The long approach on the road past his fields and pasture is about the right distance from which to get a sense of him.

We like to say that his farm is the most beautiful in Ulster County. In fact I realized lately that it's too beautiful to be accidental, just having beautiful land to start with. No. Huge, downright, and practical, Mr. Osterhoudt must be aesthetic, for many farms hereabouts have beautiful land but are coarsely kept. The road curving through his farm gives you a changing slant of light across the fields on one side and down through the pasture on the other side. The pattern constantly changes: corn rows in all stages of upright greenness, the hay field now deep in green, now skimmed, the aftermath thick with birds. But it's the oat field we slow down to see as it grows from new green to blueness, rippling in morning light, glowing bluely as afternoon melts into summer evening, until finally the blue is all used up in a ripe blondness.

The pasture on the other side of the road was Mr. Osterhoudt's own work, for it was said to have been waste land in his father's time. Its slopes and downcurves, too steep to plow, descend to a rocky stream and rise on the other side into woods. Mr. Osterhoudt's father, he tells me, was not much interested in farming—one who'd sit on his front stoop and never reach over to pull up a weed by his side. Never reach to pull up a weed, though he was sitting right there! Well, I have known many such. There are those who can look tranquilly at weeds, too small to bother with at first, mere green flecks, but growing sturdier every day, bushing insidiously right there by your knee. I admire them—the contemplators, I mean—and think how different my life would have been if weeds of all sorts didn't send irresistible impulses to my nerves.

At any rate, the pasture is now perhaps more beautiful than the fields. Its two sugar maples are the first to blaze up in the fall, and they flame gloriously even when the other sugars have off seasons. The pasture goes back into a woods thinned out into a grove. All this was dotted once with white and black milk cows, for Mr. Osterhoudt has a strong paternal affinity to these female creatures, though he is well pleased with his male heir in the human line. But dairy was unprofitable, and his son stocked the place with black beef, though Mr. Osterhoudt retained one white and black heifer.

I visit him not just to buy hay or straw but to hear his vigorous talk, his opinions of the price of seed and fertilizer, of the stupidity of government, of the best farm dog he ever had, and of a dog who though not specially smart or skilled, saved his life once when a bull charged him. The most remarkable monologue, the kind you wish you had somehow tape-recorded, was about artificial insemination, a subject we somehow strayed into as he talked about dairy cows. This was when I first noticed his delicacy, for as more and more information about the subject had to come out, he turned almost imperceptibly to address my husband, making allowances for the inescapable facts of the process he narrated by observing, "But your wife is a married woman."

Once we've got the agricultural situation well compassed, he always asks politely, "And how is your garden?" When he first did this I saw how small my place is in the scheme of things. My garden, large in my consciousness, is after all merely a garden; horticulture is a long way below agriculture.

As it happens this June Mr. Osterhoudt doesn't have any hay or straw, so I'll have to give my vegetables something less desirable. Mr. Osterhoudt's straw is very desirable indeed for, he tells me, there's no weed seed in it. I smile to myself, for a weed is not an absolute thing like a sugar maple, but only a plant you don't want. Violets are weeds to me but flowers to Shakespeare. So even when I'm lucky enough to get some of the earl's straw, some day after a rain I'll go out and see, amongst my tomatoes, oats rising from the straw of their former life, slender, already blue through their green. And I haven't the heart to reach over and pull them out.

You want to live with your garden, but you find you have to live with other creatures, like raccoons and squash borers. These are animal "weeds," but you can't pull them out. The raccoons are the most egregious. It's not that they want to live with you; they just like all your domestic arrangements, like the way you've invented the garbage can for food storage. And you can't help but be interested in their beautiful design. The babies are irresistible. You'd have to lock a child up to stop her from feeding baby raccoons and so encouraging them to domicile near your garbage can.

Then you can't help but admire their contempt for disguise. How outrageously they look the part, their bandit-masked faces turned toward your flashlight at two in the morning, just as they've boinged the lid off the garbage can and are poised on its rim, about to descend for the chicken bones. I have imagined a garbage can with a combination lock, but I knew that I would find the raccoon twirling the dial delicately with his ear to the tumblers.

Their intelligence is attractive too. My friend Molly and I once arrived at her house with a car full of staples, too tired to empty it except for perishables. In the morning, we found the raccoon had struck, devouring twelve hamburger buns and eleven hot dog rolls. His paw prints all over the windshield and side windows showed how he had kept up his research until he'd found a side vent, not open but merely unlatched. Then he'd figured out the vertical swing principle of the vent, pushed hard, and entered. We think he didn't eat the last hot dog roll because he'd made a nice calculation about how much he could stuff himself and still fit through the window to exit by dawn.

Raccoons afflict me because I have an extremely large, ancient mulberry tree. Not as great as Milton's mulberry at St. John's in Cambridge, though I may have to go to measures as drastic as the gardeners there to preserve mine. At first I didn't see the value of the tree and didn't wish it well. It shades half of the garden so that I'm put to it to think what plants can stand both its shade and its thirsty roots. It has an uncomfortable way of dropping dead limbs on the garden and perhaps on picnickers. It sends its living limbs toward the roof of the house, which stands between it and all the sun it wants. It's taller than the house, and you'd think that upper sun would satisfy it, but it's not reasonable and it favors those lower limbs. The genius who trims the tree for me won't let me clear them all because they are graceful, feathering out that way. I submit to judgment that I know is better than mine, but I gnash my teeth when my rainbow of red, pink, and violet monarda thins and starts to disappear, taking its hummingbirds with it. Still I submit, because I'm reasonable and know trees are greater on the scale of being than flowers.

The mulberry does make the yard cool in the hottest summer, leaning all its branches over the roof. The tree is a banquet for orioles, scarlet tanagers, cardinals, rose-breasted grosbeaks, and yellow finches, along with less colorful types. These birds love wild mulberries more than raspberries or blueberries, so they leave the cultivated fruit for us. Taylor says, with a kindly irony, that mulberries are food for chickens, hogs, and children. I like them anyway, and so do the wood thrush.

The tree branches extend toward my bedroom windows, the very windows from which I like to watch the hummingbirds arrive during the day. But at night the raccoons arrive. They thrash around among the branches, chomping away at mulberries three feet from my ear. The mulberries they don't get, rain—plop, plop—on the roof. And in a process that must be extremely rapid, their seed-laden feces plop on the garden and pathways. But the thing is, they fight. They growl horribly and scream at each other, especially at the babies, who make whirring noises like little clocks about to strike. When the babies get too scared, they yelp and scream in a crescendo of anxiety, perhaps for the threat to life and limb, perhaps for loss of mulberries.

Once one of these raccoons was at my mercy. I found an adolescent one Sunday morning reeling around in the roadside ditch, the victim of a Saturday night driver. I considered leaving him to his fate, thus ridding myself of him and his progeny. But the August sun was blazing down on him, and a picture of dogs finding and mauling him came to mind. He was like Satan fallen from heaven, and I was afraid to pick him up. Finally I got a moldy old coat that Leonard uses for well insulation in the winter, put on leather work gloves stiff with dried mud, and approached the beast. He hated to be picked up, but he was helpless. I put him in a screen cage built in the basement garage when it had been a country store. I gave him water, but he staggered around and knocked the bowl over. The blow from the car had evidently cracked his skull. I had to hold him in my arms like a baby and pour the water down his throat. He glared at me.

The children wanted to feed him oatmeal cookies, but he couldn't manage them. Finally I decided that eggs were the ticket, full of protein, good brain food, and liquid. My animal-loving neighbor brought me lots of eggs, which she declared she couldn't use because all had proven cracked when she brought them home from the store. I would dress in the old winter coat, cradle the poor Satan, and tip eggs down his throat. He hated me. He got well enough to eat cat food unassisted, but still hadn't all his wits about him. The beginning of school and the end of country days were near, and I didn't know what I was going to do with my boarder. But one day I went into the basement and found him climbed up the side of his cage. He gave me a hate-filled look, but I knew we were in the clear if he could climb. I thought he might rush at me when I opened his cage, so I donned my moldy winter coat for the last time. (Well, almost the last time.) He retreated. I opened the cage and the basement door and took everyone off on an errand. When we returned he was gone.

But not really, of course. After the fall he couldn't climb back into heaven, only into paradise, ready to destroy my innocent sleep. When I put on my last moldy winter coat, I'll probably meet him in another world along with my other enemies and friends.

5 : *The Genius of the Place*

I first got to know him as I toured his rock garden. He wasn't exactly there, except in his works and imagination, but I figured it was all right to walk through the rock garden because it was by the road, inviting passersby. Then I was led to the birch tree with its tiny hanging garden, to the planting fields, and the golden bantam cockerels, and the long stone table. I was reassured because I was accompanied by his golden retriever, a friendly watchdog, and watched suspiciously by his geese, who were not friendly, making a nice balance of welcome and guardianship.

A true rock garden, Leonard says, is a small-scale landscape. Aside from its plants, the pleasure of it is the way your eye alters. As the scale of everything changes, your vision enlarges and refines. You see before you the little as comprehensive and the large as comprehensible. Perry's rock garden is a New England of mild mountains and rolling valleys through which your footpath winds. There were trailing arbutus, hepatica, rose daphne, yellow primroses, and a perfectly behaved dwarf Alberta spruce, among other delights. Nothing oriental or remote, nothing painful and sublime.

I was once in on the making of a rock garden, in a humble way. My friend Molly and Leonard were scrutinizing one side of a pile of dirt and rocks that Molly and her husband were turning into a rock garden. They seemed to enjoy looking at the unmade side more than at the side Molly and Jim had completed. They looked long and occasionally uttered cryptic language. "Right there," they said, and "in that place." But there wasn't any "there" or "place." It was just rocks and dirt, and not very good dirt at that, near a shattered old rock wall. I tried to get into the spirit of the thing by gathering some nice-looking rocks that might shelve up a place to plant something, but they hardly looked at them. So I occupied myself with hauling out some of the clay to mix with peat and with sand from the children's sand pile.

After a while, they'd go over to the wall and grub around. Out would come some huge rock of an indifferent shape, not nearly as nice-looking as mine, which they'd shove into the hole from which I'd extracted the clay. "No," Molly would say. "You're right," said Leonard. Leaning on his crowbar, he looked a trifle Archimedean. Then back to the rubble to pull out an even larger and more untowardly looking rock. In went the rock. They looked at it, half satisfied, and then Leonard would seize it, give it a turn, and shove it a little. "That's it!" said Molly, and suddenly that *was* it. I couldn't believe my eyes.

"And now this other one," said Molly, and Leonard turned the other one upside down and backwards and pushed it into a place that wasn't there a minute ago. "And now over here we need something like . . ." They laughed and turned to the rock pile, as if they would recognize in it some rock, the structure of which they already had in mind for a place that didn't exist yet. They both seemed able to see the same thing in the nothing they were looking at. Occasionally they'd decided something was wrong that they had thought was right, and Leonard would crowbar a large rock out and dismantle a whole area. When the side was complete, we stood back and gazed at the little world it had become. The rocks were big, the chasms and canyons formidable. "It's the West!" said Leonard. "I think I see a posse coming through the draw."

At Perry's place I thought I saw prolific power everywhere, from the massy bluestone slab of the table with its toadstool-like seats of pipe and wood rounds to the small porous stone growing a sedum or two, hanging in the air of the birch tree, to the woods stretching away carpeted with blue myrtle flowers. Living things must spring from his fingertips, I thought. I was eager to meet him, but first I met a rich city type, locally resident. "Do you know Perry Cobb?" I said. "He must be the Genius of the Place." "Oh, Perry Cobb," he said. "We think he's a yard man." There was an unseemly emphasis on "we" and on "yard." I observed this man closely. He had a hard-jawed look. I didn't tender him any more local questions.

Perry faintly resembled D. H. Lawrence, but with humorous eyes and an eagle look about him. A kindly eagle. I consulted him about this and that, but he didn't miss anything I didn't mention. He admired my weeds, especially the purslane, my favorite. He observed the ditany and the lay of the land. He noted the old apple trees and said that if I had the patience to prune them for a few years, they would come on to bear. He said did I want to see into the woods and he would "drop" the tree that stood in my way—and did on the spot.

I could see he understood the mulberry tree with its web of huge, outlandish branches. He swung a rope over a dead limb, got into the tree neatly, saw on his belt, and said if I just pulled on the rope when he gave the word, the limb would clear the garden as it fell. It cleared the garden and me too. Leonard, who had come out and was looking at the rope with a lackluster eye, went back into the house. Since Perry seemed to understand the need for simplicity, I complained to him about the complications of the book I was studying to identify sedges and rushes. "Well," he said, "you know what they say: 'Sedges have edges, and rushes are round.'"

The rich man has died and passed, I trust, through the eye of the needle. I let the old apple trees go, but some years they bear anyway. From my study window now I see down the ridge and into the little wood, but there are things I can't see that Perry can't make spring out of his fingers, things in my way that he can't drop. There's a nothing I look at and still see nothing. I'd like to give him the little waste land beyond the wild flower garden and say, "Make me a landscape here in my image and likeness." I'd say, "I have some nice-looking rocks; I only need a place for them." But the waste land is very sandy, hardly any clay to hold a shape, and I see the tips of rocks too big for my crowbar. They are not just the loose teeth of this rocky land, I fear, but its clenched jaw. Still the Genius of the Place is not just its guardian spirit but its identity. And all I need really is patience to keep on studying the book of identities.

6 : *Catch-as-Catch-Can Garden*

You're not supposed to buy plants because you like them and then look around in your garden for a place to stick them. But everybody I know does this, though I realize I know only a humble order of gardeners. They are higher than I, of course, because their gardens are places of beauty. But gardens are also places of possibility, though possibility mitigates against beauty. Beauty has a finish to it, a perfection. It's *per-ficere,* made all the way through. Beauty pleases us with definitions, borders where the work completes itself. But my garden runs heavily on possibility, and possibility is a comic mode.

Our yearly library fair has a garden booth, and it's a great inducement to incorrect garden behavior. This year I contributed a carload of daylilies and Siberian iris—about twenty-five bags of plants—and they were all bought by the volunteer workers before the fair opened. They seemed starved for daylilies, and no wonder when local nurseries offer only things labeled "Daylily Red" or, even more ominously, "Pink." They have no Whistling Swan and Snow Goose, those pale beauties, or Kindly Light, nothing with a name to make a possibility really tempting.

I behave as badly as all the other volunteers, buying, among other things, another New Zealand primrose because it enchanted me, though I already have three. And my friends show their friendship. I'm given a red-leaf loosestrife, which I accept happily despite its warning name, and some perennial seedlings so small I can't believe they'll want five feet of space next year. When the fair is over, we two last workers face the orphan plants. How can we throw them away?

In fact I exerted myself to limit my benevolence when I spotted a young woman whom I had earlier encouraged to take some marigolds. She was leaving the fair with her two young sons, and I thought she might like a handsome young tomato plant. She was doubtful, explaining to me that she was "just renting," but then her elder son said, "Can I have it, Ma?" I turned to look more closely at this unusual young person. The family was good-looking and alert, but here was something remarkable. The boy had been paying attention, not just to the plant and the conversation, but to some original impulse in himself. It had sprung up, a possibility in the image of a fruitful young plant that needed care to complete its fruitfulness. I handed him the plant and wish now that I'd got his name.

I brought my foundlings home and parked them in the shade of the birch tree till I figured out where to plant them. This lack of method naturally betrays itself in the garden, where no sins are hidden. One long border is filled with daylilies, each with its own name, which I sort of stored there once until my plans for them ripened. I prepared beautiful soil for them and tucked them all in, feeling virtuous and benevolent. They ripened a little faster than my plans. Or my plans for them. I have a slight tendency to sprout plans, and some other aspect of the garden called on this mental power of mine and occupied it a few years.

Of course I enjoyed the daylilies in the meantime, though they are rather green all spring and fall. And when I slipped some other plants in to help these green periods, they didn't always behave well. The shasta that specifically said it was not tall, which I placed in front—judiciously widening the border a bit—looked docile the first season but then turned rank. It aspires to be a field, a four-and-a-half-foot-tall field. It's satisfyingly white, viewed from the kitchen window, and it blooms a long time, but I can't altogether see the daylilies behind it. Naturally I meditate moving it, but it looks rather defiant right now.

Normally I don't mess with seeds, but sometimes I sow them to see what will happen, and because of the opportunity for thrift. Actually the shasta was one of those opportunities. I imagine that an annual is not going to encumber the garden, but then to contradict myself, I expect good annuals to volunteer in successive years. The beautiful blue bachelor button seeded itself year after year in the worst soil in a bed I was planning to improve when I had time. The larkspur I was inspired to possess after I saw how handsome it looked in Thomas Jefferson's garden became a volunteer. And the lovely Ruby King cleome, so welcome in its excellent leaves and its tallness brightening bare places in the fall, actually comes ruby-true from seed. As you might expect, they volunteer in inconvenient places, so they are a bit of trouble. But I love their annual vigor, the way they grow hard because they know they have only a year to live. And I have plenty to give away to friends.

Then just as I got used to these annuals, they developed other habits. No more bachelor button or larkspur, except for the ones that wander behind the shasta. Only the cleome is faithful, though it volunteers late, and I notice that my friends don't need my annual progeny because they spend money on plants in May and have large cleome in June when I'm still minding my seedlings. I hope the boy who volunteered to take the tomato plant remembers to water it until it rewards him with the fruit of his idea. He's probably growing hard himself this summer, but the vigorous and pungent plant that suggested to him a new power in himself will match at least the growth of expectation, if he befriends it.

7 : *Adventitious Proliferation*

There's a good deal of adventure in a garden, in a mild way. You think of a garden as planned, and it is. Still, things happen by chance. When I first grew daylilies, I noticed one plant sprouting a tiny fountain of green leaves on the stalk. Naturally I stuck the new plant in the ground to see whether it would root and in the meantime sent off a note of inquiry to Gilbert Wild. In due course I got a postcard informing me that my new plant was an "adventitious proliferation." An adventitious proliferation! The solemn words of botany from the "Wilds of Missouri," as they call themselves. I had expected information and got language instead. Now I was no wiser than before, but I was richer by a good mouthful. I went about murmuring this mellifluous phrase to myself in a Tennysonian manner—for what is useless is free to be aesthetic.

Of course, much adventure is fantasy. You fancy that something is so, and a whole chain of causation and possibility springs to life. Then it turns out not to be so, and you're left simply with a narrative gain. But you may discover something along the way, as I found a new perennial candytuft when I was digging in the pepper bed in late May. I wasn't quite sure how it got there, but I didn't question my good fortune. I thought I must have been planning to rescue my faithful old candytuft from the deer that crop them every spring before they bloom, and I must have begun by hiding one plant among the peppers in the fenced garden. What could be more reasonable? At any rate, there it was, a stem as thick as my thumb, looking very vigorous after its spring monopoly of the beautiful soil in the pepper bed. I scooped it out carefully and replanted it in my new, fenced flower bed.

In due course it bloomed, very abundantly, and somewhat more lavenderish than I remembered it. Then a friend exclaiming over its beauty said, "But how can it be blooming so late? My candytuft has been gone for a month." Well, transplanting, the start of a new life—there are always plenty of reasons for what you think is so. Later she noticed my annual candytuft, the poor thing, growing wherever it can seed itself, in rock crevices or neglected ground, and glorifying these places with its lovely range of colors on thin stems. We took seed from an intense violet one.

Today I reconsidered my wonderful perennial candytuft. It had a familiar look. Perhaps it was really just an annual candytuft on a rich diet. But I would prefer to think that a good life transformed an annual into a perennial. I suppose Dr. Johnson would tell me, "Wonder is the effect of novelty upon ignorance," though I don't suppose he would be so strict with Shakespeare, who blithely set a play in Bohemia, "a desert country by the sea." Johnson may have underestimated the blitheness of the imagination.

The paths certainly turned out to be adventurous. The fenced garden has lots of paths because it's downhill, and the beds are terraced. These paths, naturally, are weed runs. It's no good fancying that not even weeds will grow on hard-packed, dry dirt. They do, and the worst ones grow all winter and are setting seed wildly just as you come in to look things over in the spring. Garden books have lots of advice about how to keep paths weed free, but all those ideas sprout weeds anyway. I was reading, in fact, a fascinating article on gravel gardens, and the author didn't need to assure me that things would grow nicely in gravel.

My solution, I hesitate to confess, is to put down carpeting. First black plastic and then runners cut from old carpeting that people throw out because coffee got spilled on it or it turned out to be an awful color or it's old. None of these things matter to me, though I wish more people would throw away blue carpeting. I expect the runners to rot anyway and need to be replaced, and doubtless they will. Right now they are doing something very oriental: growing moss.

First I noticed that all the runners got to be the same color, but I put it down to weathering. They got heavy too. I had noticed some moss, dank stuff, probably caffeine-tolerant, but I hadn't realized it had entirely overspread its host. It greens up when it rains, but it's gray now that a summer of no rain has turned the place into a desert. When I scraped some off to examine the state of the rug, I found the rug was its old self under there. Very odd. Symbiosis, I suppose, but who'd have thought it? I always wondered how the Japanese got all that moss to grow where garden books tell you it's so wonderful, and garden pictures confirm its beauty. I still don't know, of course, but now I don't have to.

My greatest adventure was with some morels, a fungus I was not personally acquainted with before I found it growing near the Op-Ed section of the old *New York Times* I was using for mulch. After that I found some nearly every year as the dogwood bloomed. It seemed to prefer the editorial pages, and I often thought of writing the *Times* to tell them there was more than one kind of virtue in their editorials. Then one weekend when I began to prepare the vegetable beds, I found morels growing everywhere. I felt slightly dizzy, but I knew I had to have a judicious and authoritative witness, so I called Molly to come over right away. As we gazed at scores and scores of morels we decided we'd be glad to exchange novelty for custom, but morels are adventitious, like many world events, and cannot be tamed by the application of even well-informed opinions.

The other day while doing a little meditative weeding, I almost pulled out a tiny tomato plant. It has only four leaves, but it is so vigorous it looks like a patio tomato, though it can't be, because I've never had patios in that spot. I got some very good soil from the pepper bed, slipped out the tomato carefully, marveling at its long roots threading the desert soil, and potted it. It's a beauty. Too late, probably, for it ever to have tomatoes, but I've always loved the plants when they're in their purely leafy phase, so I'll keep it to gaze at and see how it turns out. I remember reading that Tennyson used to go out in the early morning with the fishermen and chant his poems to them. I always wondered whether they really liked that. I thought I could sing about my small tomato plant to the fishermen on the sea coast of Bohemia, that desert country.

8 : "Whatever Is, Is Right"

I'm sure Pope was thinking of his gardens when he wrote, "Whatever IS, is RIGHT"—though he couldn't resist its power to outrage as the climax to one of his ascending passages about human nature. It is certainly the principle of plants ordering their own affairs in the "wild," as we like to say in our self-centered way. Places and plants normally create each other, alive on both sides it seems, so urgent is their interworking. Gardens derange this order by fixing one side. A garden begins by saying, "Place, be still!"— and then has to work with a titan's energy on one side alone. But even garden plants will work at their own cosmos. And though you might not prefer their arrangements, that's the way it is, and it's right.

I had two closed gentians in a nice shady spot near the terrace. I admitted to myself that the spot was probably too dry for them, and I didn't have an outside faucet on that side of the house. I told myself that I would see their first droop and that it wouldn't be such hard work to fetch a bucket of water from the bathtub faucet in the house, ridiculous though that might seem. They drooped often, sending me regularly on an emergency water haul, like a Prometheus too stupid to act on his own forethought.

Still they stayed with me, their bloom reminding me before I was ready for it that summer was over. The flowers really are closed, and they entertained me with the heroic struggles of their big bee visitors to pry them open, enter—and then get out again. One morning with the sunlight behind the plant, I saw in his purple bower the purple shadow of such a dauntless bee.

I figured the gentian, as a wild plant, would be enduring, but I underestimated its enterprise. One day as I was weeding the terrace stones, trying to steel myself to pull up the excesses of the wild columbine, I noticed several sets of rather beautiful green weed leaves. I spared them for a while, and they turned out to be gentians, self-sown where they wanted to be. Midterrace is not, for me, a convenient place for gentians, four of them now. But when you think of gentian seeds traveling six feet and finding a crack between stones, it would be foolish to oppose them. So I gave away their parents to a friend who has a moist rock garden, and I try to keep young human males (who tend to stride through the world without glancing down) from treading on them. I don't exactly want the lamb's ear to sprout up all over the terrace behind the gentians either, yet their wild cerise flowers angling out in a Buckminster Fuller fashion above the gray stones draw our eyes to the summer shade in a biennial fantasy of light.

The monarda is also a self-willed traveler. I want lots of it (along with its hummingbird friends) where it doesn't especially want to grow. I want the pink, the violet, and the lavender, along with the red and the watermelon one, but the pink, which makes the other colors work, is especially fugitive, except in the waste land behind the rhubarb bed (naturally). The watermelon color will take over the garden if I leave one root thread. Not to be outfoxed by monarda, I put the watermelon color in the wild flower garden where it can grow its head off and left other colors in weedy places from which I can renew my stock, I hope.

As a self-willed place a garden is vulnerable, as every gardener—or moralist for that matter—knows. A drought this year has struck my sandy soil hard, and even the wild flower garden, which harbors dry-tolerant plants, is gasping and thinning. But I noticed that in the monarda section the poor ground didn't look so bad. Apparently the monarda has been collecting fallen tree leaves, a hard thing to do here on the top of the ridge, where the November winds scour all the leaves off and away. It's quite a nice little collection of old leaves, trapped by stems and viny weeds. The monarda is making itself the place it wants despite me, its lawful gardener.

Meanwhile the phlox is moving in where monarda once flourished. Phlox is not supposed to like shade, but then, there's no knowing what it likes. It slides away from where I've planned it and gains altitude in front of a daylily or a nicotiana. One particularly adventurous phlox came to me as a sprat in the pot of some plant I had purchased. That one, whatever it was, vanished, and the deceptively gentle-looking phlox, pink and rosy-eyed, marched all over the garden. Its sports were ravishing variations of itself. Finally in its most glorious specimen, it crowned a rise of ground, pushing in right next to my handsome baby's breath. I can't move the baby's breath, because it doesn't like that, and I can't move the phlox, because it's found the right spot.

It has forced me to develop a border along the fence garden of white, rosy, wine, and purply petunias (a flower I've never especially cared for) just so we can stand at the low end of the fence and watch the pinks and purples mount up and burst into the light rose and dark rose of the phlox. I know too that having even a narrow flower bed along the fence row will make me keep the worst, wild weeds out of it. While I was at it, I thought I might as well stow my iris behind the petunias where they can spend a quiet, dry summer tending their leaves and corms. They've also spent their summer proliferating. When I had those iris where I wanted them, they sulked and harbored borers and died in a crash of heraldic standards and falls.

In the same maddening manner, the white Japanese iris, the most beautiful of flowers, huddled together and barely hung on in the perfect (though somewhat shady) spot I prepared for them. So I divided the clump, placing the extras, temporarily, in a storage bed of poor soil. Here they turned into thirty magnificent white herons, making the storage bed the showplace of the garden in early July. In a similar fashion I stored tiny, worthless, extra seedlings of achillea, "The Pearl," in a strip in front of the cucumber fence. There they flower without ceasing, weaving their vigorous green leaves into a hedge crowned with white stars. Of course the cucumbers prosper because I go down to gaze at "The Pearl" and mind the cucumber vines while I'm at it. I enjoy them together, though perhaps the combination of cucurbit and yarrow is not conventional.

This "whatever is" tendency spreads even to the buildings around the place, especially the little house by the terrace that Leonard used as a study when the children were small. Ages ago it must have been a summer kitchen. But it had gone through several cultural stages by the time I found behind it a mound of bricks thrown off, telling me that its present alcove with propane stove must have been a brick oven big enough to roast a pig. This once summer kitchen is just large enough to block any view from the terrace of the western meadow or of Venus when she glistens and dazzles and entertains her crescent sister, Artemis, or her traveling relatives, Mars, Saturn, and white Jupiter, who even in his Olympian might can't hold a candle to her.

Moreover, the inflammable possibilities of this little house are compromising the construction of a chimney on the main house. The small house is only a trifle, supported in an airy and temporary manner on layers of rock. True, it has a funny linoleum from the thirties on the floor, and its inside walls appear not so much painted as stained with blueberry juice. True, too, its white clapboards catch the full-moon light, very beautiful if you happen to look outside your bedroom window at three in the morning. Altogether it's as obstinate as the closed gentian seeding itself among the terrace stones in front of it.

It can't be got rid of. It's always been there. The huge young male who is to build the chimney, who played hide-and-seek with our children in back of it twenty years ago, and who steps knowingly around the gentians, says he still hears Leonard's typewriter tapping away inside, pausing now and then for thought. We are less headlong than the plants, it seems, and maybe still have a chance to learn forethought. Perhaps it's our sense that we know so little of "whatever is" that makes us heap up the temporary, layers as inconsequential as those at Troy till one of them filled with horse bones, telling posterity when the Trojans learned to be breakers of horses. So I must let Venus and crescent moons go and content myself, in season, with a bee in a sunlit gentian.

9 : *Denizens*

When I was a young girl I loved words like "denizen." I was a gardener of language, for I loved the roots of words. This one is from the Latin, *de-intus,* "from within, an indweller." It was a pity, I thought, that it could only be used in books and of creatures not human, though august. Whales were "denizens of the deep," and stars were "denizens of space." When my new friend asked, "Who's that little girl?" I wanted to say, "She is a denizen of my house" instead of, "She's my sister." I'm glad, however, that the creatures have so dignified an appellation.

The toad is the most worthy denizen of my garden, with a dignity surpassing my own. She seems to deplore my levity from her low center of gravity. When I'm flustered, dusting my beans with rotenone, a hateful job, and find that I've scattered some on her, she endures it as if she had expected no better of me, with a look rather like Hardy's when Laurel tips whitewash over him. Yet her weight is not just paunch but power; a ripple of leg muscle heaves her up and away. Though it's only a hop, she's out of my sight. She's a true indweller, sojourning in her thumb-size domes where the earth grains cling together over her head as if she'd mastered Coleridge's dome principle, the reconciliation of opposed forces. She doesn't recognize my boundaries and passes under the fence of the garden to the meadow, where I find her making her way back to one of her doors in the dusk.

I hope not making her way toward the snake in the garden. A garter snake, I imagine, though I never see much of this one except his elegant form and color as he moves like a live rope along edges and walls. Once in late winter I found him reclining in the middle of the basement floor, waiting, apparently, for me to come and open the doors to spring. And once, in August, I met his sinister cousin, a serpent, by the edge of the ridge. He was perhaps on his way down from the drier heights above, to the creek below. He was small, but fat and coiled. I was bare-footed and almost upon him when I saw him. I looked at him, and he looked at me. He didn't give ground. I imagined his head was triangular. He flickered his tongue, trying, doubtless, to imagine me. I got quite a good stare at him and admit he was beautiful, after his fashion. We haven't met since.

Once I was more chary of this sort of creature. A kind of very large brown spider frequents our house, a fact we discovered because the boys in our family, in the time-honored habit of brothers, liked to scare the girls by placing large, rubber spiders in their quarters, say in the middle of the bed. The joke wore out, of course, so that one sister paid no mind to the obvious fake clinging to her bedspread, until she got good and close. I was similarly startled early one morning, reaching under the sink into the dishpan to find one of these very large creatures its denizen. I called Leonard (for it's man's work to deal with large animals), and he killed it. I had wanted this, I guess, but not after it was done. My punishment was to discover later, when reading a book about spiders to the children, that there are no native poisonous spiders in our part of the world. So I learned the truth of Lawrence's poem and Eldridge Cleaver's idea that fear made me a danger to innocence, that the one who's afraid is the dangerous one.

Annoyance combined with ignorance once made me start to pluck off and discard the caterpillars on my precious parsley, though I was reluctant because they were so beautiful: vivid lime green with black and gold markings. I had to stop after the second one and let them chomp away on the tender shoots. Of course you, wise reader, know they were swallowtail butterflies incipient and will be relieved to find me confessing to no more crimes. I plant enough parsley for both of us now, and in years when the parsley is sparsely, they are happy to eat my rue.

But the beautiful creature of the garden is the golden garden spider. I wish I could claim a little sisterhood there, but she shines me down. I begin to look for her in August and spot her big web by its telltale "darning" mark. Great with her eggs, daily she grows bigger, sumptuous golden and black. She'll tackle anything, even the strong grasshoppers. They dance right into her web and are snared and trussed in a rush of terrific energy. She maps the trade currents, spanning the high tomato plants, raking in spoils like a pirate queen. Then she's gone. Her web may be intact, but is somehow lusterless, a fading rainbow of power. You'd have to be sharp to find the egg sac of her babies.

Resembling her in a way, but a foreigner rather than a denizen, is the yellow finch. There are many birds here of course, but the finch has a way of darting past the corner of the house where my study is, flashing a stroke of sunlight from his golden shoulder. It's sudden and bright, like a clap of soundless light, as if he struck the rainbow of the sun's tuning fork and found his one note.

Reading the dictionary one day, I found out that "denizen" had gone through a French phase in *denzein,* "living within," as opposed to *forain,* "out of doors." I regret the loss of *forain.* Its modern form, "foreign," isn't exotic. Certainly it hasn't the charm of "denizen," where a homely meaning sounds glamorous. Most of my garden denizens are literally *forain,* out of doors, except for the foolish mouse who wants to live in my winter kitchen, cozy under the pilot light of the broiler, bedding its babies in the insulation it pulls from the oven walls. Foolish but enterprising, snacking on the family's stock of winter squash and the birds' stock of sunflower seeds. And not even my friend Molly, clever with glass jars and metal food containers, foresaw the desperate attraction of the Crayola crayons her children left on her counter one weekend and the resultant Crayola rainbow of mouse turds: red, orange, yellow, green, blue, indigo, violet. Inarticulate in mere winter light, those mice couldn't get past the ABC of the spectrum to the white syntax of summer, not within doors, anyway.

Year Two

10 : *Herbs, Weeds, and Simples*

That hum. A sort of churning sound in the air, and I slip on my glasses to see her more clearly. Her body seems one muscle, little feet tucked up under her—so there's no air drag, I presume—though the thought of a hummingbird dragging anything, even air, is laughable. Of all the dainty or glorious flowers in the garden, she sees only the "horse mint," the coarse mint, so that we devote a quarter of the garden behind the house to it. "What is that weed in your garden?" a nongardening visitor asked once. "That's monarda," I said. "The French call it bergamot. It's quite handsome when it's blooming." I started to explain about the hummingbirds, but by that time I was seeing the monarda through his eyes, how raggedy it looked, and I thought I'd better move him on to the purple veronica. Along the way he glanced at the thyme spreading between the kitchen-walk stones. "Weed," he was thinking, and I suppose he wasn't far wrong. I don't use it often because washing those tiny leaves is a nuisance. And before I need thyme for the beans, it's gone to flower with bees making their nest under its roots, a claim I won't dispute.

"Do you cook a lot with all those herbs?" a friend asked me. No, but I idle a lot with them. I stray in the midmorning, rubbing leaves and seed pods, sniffing my fingers for the intensity of marjoram or lemon smells. In the Middle Ages, they say, babies were rubbed all over with artemisia so they would never feel the cold. I can imagine southernwood bringing summer to my skin, and that paradise had no ornamental flowers, only lemon trees and lavender.

Of course I do use the herbs for cooking as well as for pleasures more idle, but for the garden, I need them to be weedy, easy to grow and easy to use, because I'm too busy to spare time for anything but idleness. For example, we grow yards of basil so that we can freeze enough pesto base to last all winter and spring. It's dependable as a weed and more beautiful and fragrant. When I used to pick basil on one side of the house, a child playing on the other side would come around to say, "I knew you were picking basil. The smell comes over the house."

I favor the purple basil in front of the greenish-lemony daylilies. Once I had a beautiful garnish of this purple under a poached salmon. When the feast was over, I noticed that the basil still looked lively. So as a kind of comic tribute to their survival skills, I washed off the sprigs and stuck them in a water glass on the kitchen windowsill. They obliged me by sprouting roots. I potted them and kept them under the kitchen grow-light, where they cheered the winter and made themselves useful when tomato sauce was wanted.

Mints are tough, even when their foliage looks soft and luxurious, but artemisias are fussy in the north and aren't especially beautiful either. My tarragon sulks if it doesn't get the prime place of sun in the best garden—and that turns out to be not near the kitchen. But I will give it whatever it desires. Why do we want these fragrances more than color and almost more than food? Smells are more instinctive than color and more sensual, being both smell and taste. Yet they are elusive. In their presence we can recognize them, but we can't recall them in their absence. We can always imagine a color, because we have always some version of it within reach of the eye. Any patch of yellow reminds us of yellowness. Colors are abstractable. But smells are bodily, and like our bodies, both solid and evanescent.

It's said that sight relates us to the outside world and hearing to other people or other living things. So touch and taste, I imagine, link us to "lower" beings, along with that part of ourselves not easy to see or hear. I suppose, though, that we would not dispute the claim of the inaccessible to be part of ourselves. However demanding it is about sun, then, I'm thankful that tarragon is so easy to preserve in wine vinegar—as simple as steeping tea. Astringent and simple, tarragon reminds me of Artemis herself, who was never as much trouble, really, as Aphrodite or Athene.

Once the knowledge of herbs and plants—or worts, to use the old name—was essential to every medieval or Renaissance woman who ran a large, well-ordered household. She was plantswoman, pharmacist, and doctor ordinary. That wonderful old book of Anglo-Saxon lore, *Leechdoms, Wort-cunning, and Starcraft of Early England, a History of Science before the Norman Conquest . . .* , contains a trivium of useful knowledge, from spells against horse thieves to expertness in the use of plants. Nowadays, herbs are at the periphery of most unspecialized gardens. Still, most cooks use at least the bay, that subtle leaf that does not so much impart its own flavor as enable other flavors.

Weeds aren't lovable, and I see that herbs too have to "grow" on some gardeners. "I'd like some herbs," they say, "but which ones should I have, and how do you use them?" It sounds funny, like people who can't cook without recipes. You can only say, "Oh, just grow the ones that smell good to you and try them with your favorite foods," as you might say to an anxious cook, "Just add flour till it feels right."

Of course there are principles to guide experience: "Handle pastry as little as possible" or "Put in parsley by the handful." But a garden is less chemistry and more responsive life than cooking. We want to learn, and the new herb grower's question is no different than the implied question of students: "I'd like to be educated, but what books do I get, and how do I read them?" The answer is, "Begin with what pleases you. And as you go on, you'll find you are capable of pleasure more than you gave yourself credit for."

I suppose we find the balance of weed and herb, what grows for us in a welcoming way and what our hearts desire no matter how hard it is to get. The idea, as with marriage, is to discover that you want the one who wants you. And to find the combination that enables you both. We look for the best in marriage and friendship, and we make accommodations in our garden.

And thanks to my friend Marie I defy the weediness of monarda when it's not producing hummingbirds. Is it the bergamot, she wondered, that makes the Earl Grey kind of tea? Perhaps not officially, for there is a tree, *Citrus aurentium bergamia,* the rind of whose fruit yields a fragrant oil. But a few leaves of our bergamot, steeped in a pot of tea, she found, is very like, very delicious, soothes and reinstates the body's own tempo, so that we never feel the cold when we sit, evanescent in summer, out under the mulberry tree to celebrate the middle of a morning.

11 : *Naming the Opposition*

You can tell the opposition can't simply be dismissed when you find out it has names. I don't intend to get interested in them, however. They're just generic—"weeds," as most of my fellow gardeners call them. But I'm not blind to their insidious particulars. I note the cheerful green of one of them springing up from its wiry and immortal root that will run under miles of mulch to come out into air and light to choke the asparagus. Perennial rye has a white root sprouting like a tooth—the original dragon's tooth, probably—each fragment powerful enough to send up green spearmen. The more you chop it to get rid of it, the more you spread it.

One weed sports a sweet, lavender-blue flower and is named after one of those seventeenth-century minor geniuses, John Tradescant, gardener and traveler. I haven't met the higher members of its species. A blue-flowered mint creeps under the mower into garden beds to smother desirable plants. One weed looks charming for about a day in summer, delicate, tiny leaves splayed out on a stem offering white-dotted blossoms. But it's on a rampage by autumn, flings itself in a mat of seed-bearing stems all over the garden when my eye is elsewhere, flourishes in every atom of winter light, and is in full possession by spring.

Like the raccoon they are wiser and more cunning than I. They grow in their victim's space. They adopt its marks, fountaining like the daylily, lacy like the larkspur, ferny like the yarrow, feeding their wild roots next to a chosen root, stealing its summer. Every year I finally catch one that has been making me think my Japanese iris was flourishing in swords of green when in fact it was withering in the vigor of the weed. One fooled me into thinking it was a volunteer aster. I smiled at it, weeded around it, fed it with expensive fertilizer. It lay low for weeks until finally it threw off its disguise and shot up in a strong stem, budding coarse leaves with a beige flower the size of a pinhead. The sheep sorrel, on the other hand, made no bones about being anything else but simply grew virulent, smothered the grass, and choked the mower into incapacity.

At first I was surprised when I saw in the garden section of the hardware store a chart of weeds. It was as attractive as any chart of flowers. There they were, all the bad guys—root, stem, leaf, and flower: plantain, chickweed, pigweed, the lot. I was fascinated. I drew closer to study the names, both the common and the botanic, and I began to note identifying characteristics the way you do when studying a well-organized bird book. I almost wondered at so much knowledge of weeds, but I realized botanists probably know whole families in a broad-minded way, however disreputable some of the members are: speedwell can be veronica or gypsyweed. And this chart of brigands had all the impartial flavor of scientific knowledge. I almost wished I had a copy of the chart myself to get a better hold of the subject, there being a limited amount of time I have to spend in the hardware store.

But what was I thinking of? I had the villains in my garden; did I want them in my mind as well? Well, why not? They're more interesting there, and thought has a way of dis-passionating things, you might say, when passions, after all, are as unruly as weeds. The chart had been produced, I noticed, by a company that makes both fertilizer and weed killer. Across the aisle from the weed chart there was probably a flower chart. And there was the politics of the whole thing, wasn't it? "Good guys" on one side of the aisle, "bad guys" on the other.

But it was hard to say whether the chart was politicizing botany or whether the disinterestedness of science would work against the rhetoric of politics, the way those in power try to stay in power by calling the opposition devils or weeds. If I learned more about weeds, was I going to want the power to stomp them out or would I be more interested in them and begin to see them as worts instead of weeds?

In the event, I solved my sheep sorrel problem democratically. "Give the soil lime," Perry Cobb said. I told him I knew the ground was sour and had already limed it. He smiled. "I mean *lots* of lime." So lots of lime it was, until the ground was so sweet the grass decided it was worth fighting for and won. And when I looked up the tradescantias in my garden books I learned that their perfect flowers (in the language of botany) are ephemeral. You can't help but sympathize with that.

But I try not to get interested in weeds. The more names I have for what's wrong, the more time I spend on the wrong end of things. Though the weeds have wonderful common names, I need time to learn the names of the stars. Still our ancestors named weeds in a way that shows they really observed them and maybe liked them: shepherd's purse, cat's-ear, sitfast, gill-over-the-ground, lady's thumb, hawkweed, witchgrass, poor man's weatherglass, self-heal, sow thistle, motherwort or lion's-tail, love-lies-bleeding. You could compile a list of weed names from Shakespeare that would make your mouth water. How differently we look at pigweed, more-over, when we know it's amaranth. And these names and this knowledge came first, as you can tell by seeing that many Latin names are back-translations of the folk names: shepherd's-purse is *bursa pastoris* and lion's-tail is *Leonurus cardiaca*. The Shakers grew this horrid, prickly mint in their herb gardens in the belief that it helped hearts.

I might as well admit I can't resist a few of these worts. I'm thinking of viper's bugloss (*bu-gloss,* "ox tongue"), or blueweed. Bristly and coarse it is (*Echium vulgare*), but blue it is too, the beautiful blue and rosy lavender of the bluebell. And that's because it *is* a bluebell, a member of the bluebell, or borage, family: *Boriginaceae*—a satisfying, mouth-filling name with six ringing syllables. I'm going to sow some seed of it, though I wonder whether I'll regret it. I remember that Molly transplanted wild chicory into her garden once because its morning blue is so intoxicating. And once in Marie's garden I came across what was clearly a weed, growing amongst her infant tomatoes, tenderly propped by a little stake, probably for the sake of its delicate leaves and tiny white flowers. It had come to her, and she hadn't refused it.

My neighbor down the block in the city, I see, is fostering a new locust tree that has sprung up on his lawn. He's given it a sturdy stake and soft twine. I feel like warning him that it will shade out his precious rose of Sharon tree in no time. But I see that he and his wife are amiable, home-loving, and have gently raised a crop of good and beautiful children. It looks like he's one of nature's democrats, knows what he's doing, and I would do better to emulate him, in so far as I am able.

12 : *Edges*

Edges beautify a garden. In fact, the presence of a natural edge, the ridge falling off steeply behind our house, suggested at first that simply to mow the place between house and ridge edge would create the feeling of a garden. The steepness of the ridge makes it a wild world. It seems to slope away for a bit, to invite exploration. But then it drops off abruptly with an undercut, nothing between you and the stone-lined creek two hundred feet below. So the ridge stays wild, sees only the horizontal rays of the rising sun, and feels always the natural vector of rising air cool as well water.

More than anything else, it seems a different world because it keeps its own light, a light you can look into but never get into. You stand at the edge to see but never enter a remote, contiguous world with its own dappled forces in play: a fern trying to take hold, a sapling whose top leaves keep twirling in the updraft, a tree that cracked like thunder and twisted in its breaking to split all its fibers in a curved whisk. An animal trail steals along in summer, and in early spring great sheets of blue ice release themselves in a roar to drop toward the creek.

Visitors ask us why we don't "clear" some of the trees on the ridge and get ourselves a "view." We could see the horseshoe bend in our creek, view the improvements of our neighbors down on the flatlands, and there's probably another ridge looking lavender in the distance. We could see the country without leaving home, if that's a desideratum. A view would seem to enlarge our tiny backyard. As it is, they seem to say, we're hemmed in by our borders. And certainly the unimproved ridge presents a perspective we haven't designed and couldn't have imagined, a stubbornly other world right up against our own.

This edgy place attracts wild things that normally stay further away from houses. I sat up one morning the other day to see in the early ridge light two pileated woodpeckers ranging along, now flying in to help themselves to insects from my dogwood tree, now rattling away at some of the old hulks over the ridge edge. The wood thrush too seems to think the edge qualifies as woods. Early in the morning they sing in it; they may try out the mulberries or even scoot into the garden, running and pausing just like their cousins the robins. Best of all is the veery when he haunts the ridge in the evening with his song that echoes oddly as if he were whistling down a rain barrel, a long descending ripple—poignant and monotonous in the growing dusk.

I know the hateful woodchuck uses the trail, and probably so does the porcupine when he comes in at evening to gnaw on an old shed in the north meadow. It's an unnervingly loud sound, his gnawing. Once we tried to get our young neighbor to scare him with his gun. Randy arrived, the porcupine was spotlighted atop a rain barrel, huge and gnawing away at a window frame. He looked up from his work, astonished at the intrusion, apparently. Randy took aim, but the gun jammed. The porcupine took offense and ran off. Randy was so frustrated that he tore an iron fence anchor out of the ground to wield as a bludgeon, but his antagonist had fled. We decided it was better to let natural forces work themselves out apart from our efforts to pit them against each other.

Garden borders don't really keep weeds out, but a nice little run of brick, sunk low enough for the mower's wheels, gives your weeding a kind of focus. You pull out the grass creeping in, reset the bricks a bit, and somehow the whole garden looks weeded. In fact merely when Leonard mows the grass, the gardens all drifted over with hay fragrance spring into more apparent identity as garden. By a kind of exchange of perception, he weeds the garden by mowing the grass. I go out to sniff the hay air and feel complacent about my ninety-nine daylilies. The dinner guests arrive, tread the sward as if by right, smell the freshness, and say, "How beautiful your garden looks."

Raised beds, I know, are supposed to be superlative for growing things, but they rather raise the problems of edges. For my vegetable garden on sloping ground, however, they are simply a necessity. And gardening on the cheap, I propped up the "beds" by all sorts of expediencies. An abandoned telephone pole was a godsend, especially when Randy sawed it lengthwise. For the rest, I scrounged old locust posts, part of a vineyard that covered this slope once. The locust, apparently, ages into iron, for the posts must be seventy years old and show no tendency to release their hold on matter. Of course, they weren't convenient lengths, so their ends jutted across places where I wanted paths. This meant that I couldn't run a wheelbarrow freely and had to make ridiculous forays around other beds to bring compost, or lug it in by buckets to the peril of my backbone. I often wondered what the border was between my training the garden and the garden training me.

Good soil and garter snakes leaked out from under these props. The stakes I improvised rotted, and I was always jamming bits of wood or unsuitable rocks into gaps in the edging. It didn't look beautiful. Finally, to make the beds look worthy of their denizens, I invested in proper landscape ties. When Leonard and I had lugged them up the slope and sweated them into place, I brushed the dirt off their lovely flat surfaces. I had a place to set my watering can where it wouldn't get lost. I leveled some disreputable paths and embellished them with handsome old red oriental carpeting I'd saved for the right spot. The possibility of getting compost into a bed of poor soil made me lose my head and order forty-five more daylilies. The locust posts went back to the pile at the ridge ledge, where I hope they won't encourage the woodchuck to burrow and set up household within hiking distance of my ripening tomatoes.

But it's still Leonard's mowing that makes the borders look beautiful, I notice. At the end of the mown meadow the wild flower garden in June looks wild with pleasure. And the writers and readers around the place still prefer to set their chairs at the edge of the ridge and rest their eyes in glances at the undisturbed slope, the tops of trees below, and some fugitive glimpses of light on bits of the creek.

Up close, edges melt into transitions, ways of getting through borders to a different light. To see the ridge properly, you'd have to leave it and go to the far end of our land by the road. From there you can see the whole line of very tall locusts on the ridge edge, and as you walk toward them, they seem to mount up the slope of the ridge till they stand behind the house. Their structure is the ridge shape, transposed into the air where you can see it better than when you're standing on it. The locusts are so airy and lightly branched that when you stand under them, you can sense their altitude only in June about nine in the evening when the last of the light is still up there on their fragrant blossoms, and the bees are thickly humming, industriously draining the last sweet drop of the day. Apparently it's distance that makes the real edges spring into view, they being the gift of perspective.

13 : *Orientation*

People who've never really been in the country are most surprised by its darkness at night. "It's so *dark!*" they say in disbelief, as if darkness weren't an ancient, long-enduring experience, well attested in the human record. "So *dark!*" they repeat, as if there were no other words for it. And sometimes they add, "Aren't you ever afraid?" Though we laugh, their *frisson* is wonderfully expressive. We know that the darkness of country nights is as precious as its fresh air.

Every night it comes, not just a matter of the sky, but a feeling all around, like a meta-silence, a fifth element, more bodily than air, more humanly habitable than water. In it a different dimension of our senses comes forward. Sight modulates. We learn we can see in the dark and move around familiar territory. In fact sight shifts away from its analytical mode to become something more elemental, an easy confidence in the familiar, a being widely at home. Contrary to our instincts to take flashlights into the dark with us, we need sight less at night, because then it gives up the lead and falls into a lively, working fellowship with our other senses. Then we realize that our whole body is one delicate sense, creating at every moment the outline of energy of the other things in the world.

Some people want night-fragrant flowers, as if one needed little here-and-there rewards for a night stroll. The moonflower shimmers its great white fabric, unfolding into an exotic smell. The night-blooming cereus is a fantasy with its huge flower and all those white and gold stamens curving thick as the breast feathers of a heron. But these plants are really tropical and keep their longing for the south. In my garden most of their buds are killed by frost. If late summer lingers, however, you can troop out with a flashlight to see the cereus at midnight, an exotic treat for visitors and children.

But the ordinary pleasure of night is simply to see the stars or the moon in her phases. We used to set up for a full-moon rise in the summer, lining up garden chairs as if we were on deck, providing blankets and pillows, passing out children to spare laps, and waiting, giddy as luxury-liner passengers, for the old galleon to heave into view. We tried to see colors, and we told each other that in January, when the moon is much higher than it is in summer, we could read a book of poems outside if we had gloves warm enough. It was odd to walk down the road and see the woods, so dark in the daytime by contrast with the road, opened and lit by moonlight.

We wanted to learn the stars, but though they seemed close on a crisp winter night, they were as remote from our ken as all the poems say they are. Television nature programs were of no use because though they reveal much about nocturnal animals, they can't shine lights on the stars. Lectures are artificial, and books are tiresome because they prefer to give stars numbers rather than resonant names. What right have they to interfere with the continuance of mythology? And of course it was maddening not to be able to read a star chart by flashlight at night outdoors where it would do some good. There they were, our own sublime, burning and prodigal in the vastness and deeps of the skies, but which was which?

Not that we were completely lost. We had heard, "Arc to Arcturus," and had followed the arc of the Dipper's handle to find the rosy diamond of Arcturus, very satisfactory in May. To be sure, it wasn't hard to follow the arc further to Virgo and Spica, that fierce virgin, Astraea, and her star. As Astraea, or Justice, was the last of the gods to leave humankind, lingering with us through the Golden Age, it was good to find her and see in her our vernal hope for her return. True too the giant Orion, the most beautiful constellation, was easy to recognize in the brilliant cold of winter, striding across the sky with his two great stars saying in Arabic that they are Betelgeuse, "on the Giant's shoulder," and Rigel, on his "foot." This happy association of Greek giant with Arabic names reminds us how we in the West owe to Arab scholars the preservation of Greek learning in our Dark Ages.

We knew that Orion was following the Pleiades and that we therefore had not far to look for Taurus and the excellently bright Aldebaran, whose Arabic name tells us he too is "the follower" of those enchanting sisters. No, we were not deprived. Orion gave us Sirius, the brightest star in all the heavens. And though ridge trees obstruct my view of Venus when she is *stella splendida, et matutina,* the bright and morning star, I get good light from her in years when she is Hesperus in the early dark of winter. But, except for Venus, the planets' wanderings were hard to follow. And we couldn't just learn all the stars separately. So far it was the shape of myth that guided our steps, in so far as we took steps toward the stars in the dark at all.

Then we found out about the line of transit. I knew some simple principle would open our perceptions. All I needed to do (almost) was find south, and I'd already found that. When planets or stars crossed that imaginary line between east and west, they were crossing the line of transit. Then there were plenty of charts to tell us when a constellation or planet was transiting in a certain month at a certain time of night. If a particularly beautiful configuration emerged from the wheelings of space even at four-thirty on a cold winter morning, as happened one year when Saturn, Mars, and Jupiter lined up in a glowing arc with Antares, I could get up to see it.

It was a matter of orientation, another example of a principle I'd known all along, but forgot to trust sufficiently. We had always noticed that the flaw in most houses is not their interior design but their lack of orientation, their failure to know the east and face the best of their windows south. The architect of our own old winter house, in a fit of professional incomprehension, had lined the south wall with plumbing and stairways and gone off into eternity leaving the house to face the north as best it could. Certainly we humans sense our own capacity to work best when we place ourselves in an unobstructed line with our source powers.

So orientation must be deeply personal. Old persons especially want to keep hold of where they are psychically: "at home," though they mistake their present physical location. It's odd that we speak of the old as "disoriented" when they are not lined up with us. Maybe they know where their east is, and we are not lined up with them. The psyche is probably the self-piloted sense of a line of transit between rising and setting from which you can identify certain configurations in their time and season.

In his extreme old age, my father, cared for in my house, was at his best when he had placed himself "at home" and welcomed us as his guests. He inquired whether Leonard had everything he needed, urged him to help himself and even spend the night if he wanted to. Rightly oriented, he was free to practice generosity, a congenial mode, evidently.

In our night excursions we were trying to make ourselves free in the fresh air of the dark and learn more about it. Planets and stars are there in the day sky, of course—something that never occurred to me when I was a child. But for us personally stars are part of the dark because we need the dark to see them. No matter how north our city winter was, in the country we had open views to the south and a chance to find some principle so we could get our bearings. With that, even though planets are wanderers without houses, we can welcome them when they come our way. In the meantime, the dark is there to be felt. A flashlight could hardly improve that experience.

14 : *History*

We bought this land and house from a woman named Hyacinth. She smiled kindly at me and said there was good timber on the ridge, "if you can get it out," and that I would probably want a dog to "walk over the place." I couldn't see any way of using her counsel at the time. I had already ventured thoughtlessly over the ridge edge and realized how easily I could slide over the drop-off into eternity. I wasn't going to send anyone else over to get out timber that had much better be left to keep the ridge from eroding back to the house. As for a dog, we planned to live there only in summer, and I considered I had a sufficiency of children to feed and exercise. Still it's never wise to dismiss what an experienced person tells you, so I kept the notion of exploiting the ridge somehow. And I turned over in my mind a new idea: that a place needs to be "walked over."

It took a long time to settle in—about twenty years, I suppose. There was more of it, you might say, than there was of us. There were layers of lives, house ways, culture, American history to learn, from the nutmegs in the kitchen to the wringer washing machine in the bathroom to the mower with reciprocating blades in the basement. Some places I couldn't excavate for at least ten years, like the closet in the bathroom from which I took broom, dust pan, mop, and put them back without going deeper into its mysteries. It did contain a wonderful glass scrub board, thankfully immune to rust, along with a good wooden ironing board. It was easier to possess ordinary skillets and plates, even one oddly shaped bowl that someone finally figured out was pig shaped. It became the "piggy bowl," a favorite for snacks.

It wasn't that the place contained marvelous antiques or natural wonders, though the real estate agent implied that our borders enclosed a waterfall. It was the poor house of ordinary country people living on mighty poor land. In fact when I wondered why the floor was so bouncy in front of the stove, I took out four layers of linoleum to find—that I had been standing on four layers of linoleum. At the back of a dressing table drawer I found an old report card for a boy who had received A's in all his subjects and was yet failed in his grade because—the impersonal teacherly handwriting said—of "excessive lateness." This was very painful. I held it in my hand for a long time, seeing the boy's shame, the parents' helplessness. Hyancinth Miller was a woman of color, and I couldn't help but wonder whether the boy's color had blinded somebody.

There were other signs to read, like the metal numbers over the doors of the rooms upstairs, going back to the time at the turn of the century when the house had been a rooming house for workers on the reservoir pipeline. "The bathroom is number two!" the children gleefully reported. The barn had changed from a place to store hay to a place to raise chickens, with windows let in to give them light. A pad of notepaper in the basement said, "Lay Or Bust!" A hand-lettered sign read, "Asparagus for Sale." There were remains of pigpens on the rocky slope above the barn—built in fact on her property, a neighbor told us.

I had already spotted signs of the asparagus bed. I could hardly believe my good fortune; there seemed to be three rows thirty-six feet long. Molly and I were examining it when a neighbor appeared to say, yes, it was still alive, and we would have a "superabundance of asparagus." Molly informed him that there was no such thing as a "superabundance" of asparagus. From an earlier era of the place, more oriented to beverage, there were a vast grape arbor on a south-sloping meadow and large old apple trees. Still earlier was the stone foundation of the tiny house across the road and the stone cistern on the slope behind that house, built just inside the property line to catch water from the spring across the border. It must have been the original water of the place and it, like the land for the pigpens, was borrowed.

Down the road, in a tavern belonging to the first owners of our place, there is a photograph taken in 1913 of our house as the "Central Hotel," the proprietors lined up in front, in the long white aprons of the store or cider shop they operated in the basement. Now named Brown, they were once, in another country before they became liable to the rust of the American monosyllable, named di Domenici. The Central Hotel in all its tininess must have been a boarding house, a domestic counterpart to the great aqueduct, which runs like a raised highway through the woods across the road, the stone of its viaducts chiseled "BWS, 1908."

Down the road in the opposite direction is an empty stone cabin, scrupulously bare, inhabited once in summer weather by a famous philosopher, who would arrive in a station wagon topped by her canoe named "Creek Mouse" and who wrote about art and form by lamplight. She turned out to have been the actual owner of the pig pens and the waterfall. Now that she is fully in eternity, the place is unlit. But Leonard and I cleared her cistern of leaves anyway and replaced its cover.

We learned the dishes by drying them, the dresser scarves by ironing them, and the land, it turned out, by walking over it, finding shattered old quarries and pastures grown over with woods. This is hard land; it drove out the enterprises that cleared it and closed in after them. The tiny Revolutionary War stone house down the road has its stone floor finished with three or four gravestones its owner had prudently carved for his family ahead of time. But he found he couldn't afford anticipation and had a prior and daily use for them. He may have thought that as the named stones were required by their namesakes, they would be called forth by those who needed them more, as the house needed them less. There were some successes in the region, some large stone mansions, but it's said they were built by slave labor, and there's no blessing on them.

Still there's always the impulse to go against entropy, even though you know the stream runs down faster than you can swim up. We demystified the bathroom closet, throwing it out along with the bag of old clothespins in its depths to make room for an automatic washer and a dryer. I recovered the ironing board, bleaching the nice old hotel towels I found being used as its pad. A few stubborn stains yielded to the scrub board, and now the towels are sacred to drying hair. We too began by borrowing, letting our friend Jim Finn finish rooting out the grapevines—wild and thick as old apple tree limbs—when Leonard broke his arm.

The house itself yielded tools for its continuance: a crowbar, the old mower that sliced through years of wild weed tangle. But we couldn't stave off all losses. The asparagus bed was finally routed by age, tree roots, and shade. In the dining room a charming window pane "frosted" with a beer advertisement was broken one winter by real ice built up outside. Still there was a kind of balance. The barn, which Molly's mother said was an eyesore, finally fell down, relieving the aesthetic burden on the landscape.

Hyacinth's grandchildren come back as they grow up, wistfully looking things over and explaining to their companions how things were. One of them left me a card offering to buy the place back if we ever wanted to sell out. I always felt apologetic about our changes, so I was cheered to think he wasn't going to let them stand in his way. A friend went over the ridge, despite my warnings, to search for old bottles. He found some, but he is a connoisseur, and none were worthy of his collection; so I get to dust them and consider their archaic forms and less than symmetrical art. Remarkably, nutmeg doesn't lose its savor. I make sustaining custard in Hyacinth's custard cups, which look just like my mother's, and I grate a little softly fragrant nutmeg on top in the old way.

15 : *Country Children*

We bought the country house for the sake of the children, though they weren't always grateful. We couldn't afford to send them all off to camps in the summer. Besides, we didn't want to part with them, since they were always at such interesting ages. So the children liked the country or didn't like it, but there wasn't anything they could do about it. Free from school, they learned or didn't learn what they were looking for, without the benefit or hindrance of teaching.

There was one exception: swimming instructions at the township beach on the creek. Lessons began at nine on cold summer mornings, and I was keen to see how Pete, the head lifeguard, would manage them. The poor, skinny little six year olds were hugging themselves, quivering with the cold, eyeing the chilly gray water with sinking spirits. I put on my sweater. Pete arrived looking jovial, but he couldn't fool us. He backed into the creek. "Okay," he yelled. "Splash me! Go ahead! You're allowed!" They couldn't believe their ears. Splashing the lifeguard was heinous, banishment its consequence. They waded in to get him, at first hesitating, then laughing, yelling, getting their heads soaked. It was a prime demonstration of teaching. He had figured out that the first step in swimming is to go into the water, and he got them to take it.

The children were to progress each year through Red Cross–approved stages till they reached Lifesaver status. All of our children did except Matthew, who developed porpoise tendencies and didn't bother to put his head out of water and breathe properly. This was a puzzle, because he could undoubtedly save lives in his own porpoise fashion and he didn't claim badge or certificate. But well-run (or swum) systems don't easily tolerate unofficial salvation. So the affair was compromised along existential lines when he passed the test by saving in his own way the largest and most determined-to-drown lifeguard and was allowed to save lives thereafter at his discretion.

The beach seemed to be as close as the children got to "country." And really most of us adults thought of the country in a relaxed way as a quiet place to read. For swimming we preferred the beautiful pool of the creek two hundred feet down the ridge behind the house, though we may not have been ready for the full naturalness of it. Chest deep in the water there one day, I was startled to see a large black beast swimming toward me. I sensed my uncertain footing, my incomplete swimming ability, and the isolation of the place. The question of when the last wolf was seen hereabouts occurred to me. The animal turned out to be an intelligent Newfoundland, awfully glad to be meeting friends in her lonesome afternoon.

Later, as I talked with young Hannah, a five-year-old visitor, we saw the dog emerge from the woods, the ridge having proved no obstacle to friendship. Earlier that summer Hannah had announced that she was deathly afraid of dogs. Now I could feel her prickle. "What's that?" she said. My heart sank. "That," I said, "is a bear. A nice, friendly, black bear." Hannah relaxed. She was of course more familiar with bears than Goldilocks had been, and she greeted the animal without prejudice.

At frequent intervals all summer long the children would tell us they were bored. We told them to go out and unlock the secrets of nature, like the children on the television we had left in the city. But even visitors from down the road or across the road would tell us they were bored, an exasperating announcement when eleven or twelve children are going though gallons of milk and loaves of bread, making peanut butter sandwiches in your kitchen, which is twenty miles from a grocery store. In the intervals of boredom, however, they invented entertainments for themselves.

They played Monopoly in the middle of the living room floor, a maddening practice because the floor really only had a middle—the room was ten feet wide. So they seemed to understand the meaning of Monopoly all right. Monopoly lasted for ages because they compromised the rules—giving large sums for passing Go, for instance—to save those who were sinking into ruin. They realized the bank would run out of money and considered printing more themselves, but decided that would be cheating. So when bank funds ran low, there was a general levy.

They had figured out that the game was most interesting in its first half when everyone was acquiring property, traveling freely along the infrastructure provided by the manufacturer, improving settlements, and praying for a little bad luck for their friends and relatives. The older ones, having learning how to pronounce "Reading," could snub the younger ones. They saw no need to face the pain of the game's second phase of ruin and bankruptcy, where the original settlers, lucky in their landings, raised rents while their victims wept, turned into bad sports, and resented poverty hysterically even though there was plenty of peanut butter in the kitchen. They simply kept on with the first phase of capitalism till they got tired of it and quit.

Some entertainments were places they imagined for themselves. We didn't have a couch, but a single bed under the window in the living room became the couch, and the children took it over. Any number could read on it, piling up pillows, quarreling with anyone who read aloud from a book someone else hadn't read yet. For a time the younger boy occupied the bed-couch to recuperate from a foot injury. He read through the works of Flannery O'Connor, which seemed an odd choice for a thirteen year old. We kept puzzling over what he could be getting out of them. When the bed-couch broke a leg, the children propped up the corner with bricks, which toppled periodically. The bed finally broke altogether, but to this day the children remember its removal as a reproach to the parents who discarded it rashly.

One year I was startled to discover that the girls were playing a game called Mean Mother. When I tried to inquire about it casually, their attention melted away. The evasion made me feel worse. My heart was smitten at the thought of all the power we have over children and at the idea of all my sins as a mother reenacted by children who were too smart by half.

When I finally overheard the game, it was this: Daughter, locked up by Mean Mother, tries desperately to meet Boyfriend. Nothing more. Over and over she tries to escape, aided by Friends through whom she sends and receives notes, and is dragged remorselessly back by Mean Mother, whose vigilance has been distracted by Friends only for a moment. The plot repeats endlessly, stirred into life by a single force, the obdurate meanness of Mother. Boyfriend never so much as locked fingers with Daughter before Mean Mother snatched this struggling young girl back into the safety of her room.

But there was apparently some exploring of nature, though we were unaware of it. Leonard was surprised one day, as he ran along the pipeline through the woods, to look up at a steep rock outcropping and see his ten year old clinging to rocks and branches halfway up, unable, evidently, to climb further or come down. Leonard paused to pluck him off and set him back on the ground before he resumed running. "But how long had he been up there?" I demanded when he told me the story later. "I've no idea," he said, an answer I should have expected, for Leonard was never one to inquire minutely or impertinently into the affairs of others. Probably most children's explorations are, like this one, in the country they imagine, beyond our ken, first steps into a water we have forgotten.

Year Three

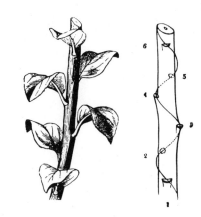

16 : *The Brink*

The first of May is the brink here in the foothills of the Catskills. Spring actually began long before May. From behind our windows in March we could see the tree buds swell week by week. We could imagine the sap rising, the skunk cabbages burning their way through snow, and the jack-in-the-pulpit unfurling its curious calyx. The wild plants all hurry out in the cold and muck before we care to go out to see them, and before the trees flower. When tree leaves are fully out, summer takes over, and spring has gone. But in between, in this moment, spring is about to spill over into its full rush.

In early May there's a new downpouring of light; yet you still have the in-sights of winter. You see deep into the woods, see the contours of the land: dips, scrapings, risings into stranded boulders poised on rock ridges—and the ridge falling into water courses. You seem to see what the ancients saw in the land: recumbent giants, downcast but in Antaean power—their hip bones, shoulders, and flowing, indented spines.

And you see this structure through a dotted filigree of greens. The mono-green of summer is another four or six weeks away; now every tree shows its own red, green, or golden kind. The light pours through the whole delicate network, a glinting refraction of tiny, perfect leaves, too minute to baffle your gaze. You understand what the Greeks meant by *charis:* the visible, inalienable grace of a thing. Not a golden haze but the articulated network itself: every leaf, the upsurge of trees, the inertia of boulders, the rolling away of the land.

Early spring is the heyday of the "garden-keepers," the plants that get going long before I have my garden wits about me. Rhubarb comes stoutly up in April, its leaves looking like something Hokusai peasants use as umbrellas in the rain. (A dish of pink and green rhubarb sauce, I felt when I was a child, cleansed my bloodstream of winter.) Asparagus tips mark the first day of May promptly. The little red poppy seeded itself and has come up in the grass and amidst the lettuce. Larkspur and bachelor's button are way ahead of my spring efforts.

Some of these plants were infants in late fall and survived the winter—hard to believe if you think of annuals as too tender for northern winters. In fact there are plants simply averse to summer, like poppies and grasses. In their perennial form they estivate in hot weather; as annuals they die in summer, germinate in autumn, hold on through winter, and are going strong in the spring before we hibernators have shaken the sleep from our eyes. And all are beautiful like the chervil, a fine lacy green over otherwise waste places.

My friend Molly gave me my first stalk of chervil netted with shiny black seed and advised me that once it got started, I would never have to sow it again. When its remnants occupy summer ground inconveniently, I lay the seed-laden stalks behind perennials and especially under the shady junipers where nothing normally grows but weeds. It sprouts in fall, and by spring its green leaves lace the shade. In summer the leaves bleach to linen tinged with rose, beautiful ghosts under the dusky junipers. Finally it all turns violet and hangs out stalks fretty with black seeds. I'm grateful that it finds its way around the garden like a weed, but better looking, more reasonable, and better tasting on chicken and fish.

But I hardly get to use the chervil, it's so much earlier than I am. It signals spring steadily, but I can't get to the garden because my job is urgent in spring. May, the best of months, slips past me, all its glories of magnolia, dogwood, azalea, candytuft, and tulips gone before I can give them an hour of good, quiet looking.

In this season I appear, even more than usual, a careless gardener. Once during a spring house party of some of my daughter's friends, a young professional gardener got up in first light, I'm told, to inspect the garden. His report: "It's the serious garden of someone who probably hasn't had time to do her spring work," a charitable restraint when his eye fell on wild ramps, a jungle of jewelweed, an invading army of rye, perennial seedlings thick as stars, the tail end of daffodils, and only the dogwood in bloom. Still, he gathered heaps of chervil when it was his turn to prepare a meal and took a seedling of dictamnus back to try out in Virginia. Would he had carried away a dozen!

But he must have noticed that the gardener had stirred herself early to sow lettuce. Even in an April downpour, if it's the only moment you have, you sow lettuce for the joy of daily salads later. In mid-May it hadn't yet become what Leonard calls my "lettuce hedge." I don't believe in thin sowing in rows I'll have to weed later, thinning again, waiting for a commercial-looking head to harvest. "Use the thinnings in salad," they say, but what a pitiful salad that would be. They don't know that our family needs, for salad, a quart of lettuce for every two people. Blood meal and plenty of water keeps my "hedge" coming so that we can clip a portion of it straight across every day, and it doesn't have time to think about bolting.

Thoreau, always celebrating earliness, said Hebe was the giver of youth and the daughter of wild lettuce. That was in the youth of our country and in his own youth in a century when a lot of youth didn't live to grow old. But maybe if you're not good at earliness, it's enough to cultivate your lettuce and catch glimpses of Hebe in the unencumbered light. In early spring I let these greens keep my garden for me, and to visitors I imagine serving a light native repast of lettuce and chervil salad followed by rhubarb pie.

After all, I am myself busy with the young in May. I cultivated them pretty well in winter because they were already on the brink when they came to me. They were emerging into their own various greens way ahead of the buds we could see swelling outside our classroom window in the clearing rain. Always hungry, they bolted out of class toward lunch, leaving me their umbrellas, no more bothering to reclaim them later than if they had been rhubarb leaves.

I look for plenty of flower and fruit from them by the end of May. Here, as in my garden, I expect Nature to make up my deficits, and in spring and youth she does it generously. I didn't sow them, and I don't care whether they go off to estivate after the spring harvest. But in the downpour of early light and with the insights of winter I see the outlines of their power. After they've gone I look at my collection of umbrellas, a device I never use, and think whether I might take a contemplative stroll in my garden in the rain to view my weeds in their glory.

Places are more often found than planned. On my first walk through a friend's house I realized that it felt enchanted because it was full of places— nooks or embrasures where you would like to be for a while and where you felt purely some original self. The house had been made out of a barn—out of necessity, before such things were fashionable and slick magazines told you how to do it—and made by a man whose character you could feel in his making. Constructed I suppose on the principle of the afterthought, or of developing need and possibility, it has one or two large-minded but perhaps inconvenient features—one has to go through a bathroom on the second floor to reach the master bedroom, for example.

A ladder in this bedroom leads to a sort of extra floor and a small suite of rooms that are still speculative, but lovely and bare like an eyrie. In fact the second floor itself is so far above the main floor that it suggests a different sort of life, less public and reachable, more individual than main-floor life. There seems to be an indeterminate number of bedrooms, some of which are entered almost by conundrum, since you must find access to them somehow from the second-floor balcony, which wraps around the open shaft going up through the center of the house. My favorite place, in a corner of this wide balcony, is a bed-couch piled with pillows where I could hide away from chores and read all day or stay up till all hours reading in the glow of my own lamp while other people found their way to their bedrooms. It's a house that gives place to its inhabitants.

I think there's no theory of anticipation for places. You probably can't build a house or plan a garden so they will sprout enchanting corners. Places appear out of the big structure you're working with, something given and necessary, like a barn or language or watercolors, and you develop them by recognition. I remember at Hatfield House a stone garden seat that had covered itself with wooly thyme. Perhaps someone designed the seat so she could sit and look at a border of flowers and then discovered the sense of floating on thyme, wrapped in the sturdy fragrance of thyme so that simply being there was enough in itself.

Those English painters of the early nineteenth century understood this, those who didn't rush off to paint something already there, like the Matterhorn or the Jungfrau. They saw places full of feeling where no one realized there was a place at all. Constable found the landscape in the Vale of Dedham, where he could see the clouds and water mills of his childhood, and Cotman painted a knoll on Mousehold Heath where you could lounge and turn your back on the tracks below as they converge and then run away to the corners of Norwich. The garden at Vézelay is hardly remarkable as a garden, but it is what it feels like to be a pilgrim, to have mounted up and then be able to look round 360 degrees.

The places in our own house are there, I think, by relating you to something outside—the sun or what it lights on. Originally there was one small window in each room; now there are ranks of them inviting you to turn outward or at least let light in on your work. At the front of the house, even on the first floor, you are way above the road, superior to all those strangers rushing rootlessly along. But at the back you are tucked into the ground, below the level of the yard and intimate with the ridge. In the kitchen you are almost outdoors, even when you have a day's work ahead of you at your desk. One step carries you into some garden place and away from the dinner dishes. It also carries dirt and grass clippings back in onto the kitchen floor. So the easiness of the outdoors has its intrusions, but we're willing to sweep them up.

Upstairs, lounging in the east-south window of my study in midmorning, I seem to be in a basket of dappled light spread by the sun behind the birch tree whose sparkling shadow on the grass is a dial curving as dark-green shade and light-green light, its trunk the gnomon describing the arc of the morning. The rue is in full sun, but its imbricated, deeply cut leaves speckle their own bluish light-and-shade in and out of the clump, their yellow flowers waving above. Light flickers over the deep coral daylilies and beams on the open countenance of the lemon one. This is the most beautiful place, but whether in the house or in the garden, it would be hard to say. It isn't really there unless you're seated and looking down through the window that frames the sunny air.

Behind the daylilies a rock wall begins and rises with the ground above the first floor. Against that wall I thought tall rock rue would look beautiful and be close enough to pass every time I went out, sure to see the dew and rain they hold in diamond drops on the surface tension of their leaves. When they seeded themselves on the bed above the wall to rise above my head, I almost transplanted them, but Leonard advised against it. He was right. Now from up here, as the climax of the light, I see their glowing sepals, a cloud of tiny purple spheres apparently afloat in the air above the rising stone wall. They seem only a step away from the illumination of the air itself.

The small bird feeder in the birch is a center of liveliness, echoing the liveliness of the plants in the light. When I arrive in the country after an absence, and the feeder is still, I feel the lack of life and movement with a pang. What I want is not so much showy birds but the feeling of energy at work in a world where I can confide in it. I want especially the chickadees' dipping flight, their fearless approach right past my shoulder, and the racket they set up in the morning if we haven't got the sunflower seeds out early enough.

The stone wall curves around, trying to keep the earth away from the back wall of the house. Apparently an extension along the back of the original house was just scooped into the hill, whose earth then bowed in this new back wall. This was amended by scraping out a corridor between house and hill, retaining the hill by a heavy stone wall as high as my chest. I fear it gets less solid with the years. Even now it's porous enough to house a woodchuck who wanted to live near the tender garden shoots—very inconvenient from my point of view and hard to sweep away. The lower part of the wood wall of the house was replaced by a cement wall, which had to make a bow to concavity because by that time the house was permanently bent. But then, as Leonard complained when we bought it, there isn't a right angle in the house, amid all its meetings of walls, ceilings, and floors.

Though the dining room is darkly east-north, the garden just outside and half way up its windows is reaching for the light. Looking through the glass of this dim room at all the light and color on the other side gives you, as Leonard says, the feeling of being in an aquarium. Insects and an occasional hummingbird hover around larger fish, the monarda and daylilies, all swaying in their currents. It's the coolest place to work in the summer, but I find its aqueous light a trifle exotic.

The height of this garden outside the dining room puts it only half a story below my study, which is a shed dormer, pushed out under the roof to make the bedroom of two little girls a more tenable space. Now that they're grown, it has become mine, a kind of hand-me-up, like the clothes I get from them when the style but not the use has gone out of them. Had I planned a study, I would have faced myself full south. As it is, most of my windows face east-north. This might not have pleased me once. But I've learned that the flowers I look down on are reaching for the south, and so they keep turning toward me as if I were their sun.

I seem to be in my own eyrie up under the mulberry, watching the bugbane whose Latin name, *Cimicifuga* (*cimex,* "bug" + *fugare,* "to put to flight"), tries to imitate its English. Its names please me almost as much as the plants do. They were a donation and an experiment; now they are a success, raising up a dozen, seven-foot white wands, vigorous spooks in the shade. I notice that the accident of having placed a rather ordinary daylily where it gets dappled afternoon light reveals that its flowers are chalice-shaped. If I had devised my place instead of falling into it by necessity, I probably could not have anticipated so many occasions for self-congratulation.

I'm at the right distance to overlook the willfulness of plants: the way the cerise phlox volunteers next to the peach daylily, and the coneflower crowds the yard side of the garden, hiding everything behind it from anyone in the yard. From my point of view, however, the coneflower leans toward me, by way of the snowy shasta, the violet monarda, and the gold daylilies. I see my errors rectified by the sun—the errors of my garden, that is. As for the house, still not right-angled, it has to be content with owners who think home improvement is filling walls with windows. Through my enlarged window I can see the birch-bole gnomon telling me that the morning is getting on faster than my studies. I learn that places are the accidents of necessity and given by grace. Too rooted to be a pilgrim, too limited to see all around, in my study I'm only a little taller than my usual self, trying to turn garden into language. And by trial and error—or by grace and favor—I've found a place to get on the right side of the sun.

When I go into the depths of some redolent old bookstore or second-hand shop with my friend Marie, it's partly to look for the results of her genius for finding a choice artifice, like the little white Limoges cow for pouring milk onto your oatmeal or fine percale pillowcases deep with hemstitchery, something sent into the world a second time that hasn't yet been noticed. Not even a leather-covered *Webster's New International Dictionary*, Merriam Series (priced at nine dollars), is as conspicuous as you might imagine, for the sight of a great big book makes some people avert their eyes from the labor of opening it.

Her findings are the light-hearted expression of an instinct at work in a delicious, recurring dream we both have of finding a cache of neatly ordered supplies always in place. Hers is the dream of a cupboard with shelves piled with linen paper, a pair of sharp shears, and drawers with rolls of French silk ribbons of all widths in lemon and cream and deep rose and blues and sparkling, vivid greens of all shades, in grosgrain, satin, moiré, or pure texture of silk. I recognized the wish fulfillment in this dream the first time I heard it, for no woman with children will ever find sharp shears during her waking hours.

The remnant of linsey-woolsey, the blackened but sterling serving spoon suggest that some lost good can come to light again. And now someone has found the place down the road—or rather someone has found it for keeps. Of course we had all found it, especially the children, who were charmed by the pond or by the simplicity of its little brown-shingled, two-room house with its sky light from a southeast dormer. They used to talk about buying the place when they grew up. The house is set in the open on the far, upward incline of a bowl of rocky land, at the bottom of which is a trapezoidal pond with stone-set sides, which made the land a small walking-to place in spring for parents of little children.

There we watched floating salamanders eat floating frog eggs and spied the elder frogs themselves. There Leonard spotted the only spring peeper we've ever seen among the hundreds of thousands we've heard. And there as we lay on our bellies on the cold stones to peer into the pond, we recognized that what we first thought bits of debris were actually "litter bugs," creatures stuck all over with a disguise of pond litter, moving slowly along underwater stems. Actually they are the larvae of the caddis fly, and later we saw their trick of sliding out of the water, transformed, to dry their wings and fly off.

Its owners mowed the place on their once-a-year visit, but it never looked overgrown, an odd fact that Leonard observed every year as he mowed his own tirelessly growing meadow. Once the owners told me to take some of the gooseberry bushes disappearing in the shade of a fast-growing fir. In return I picked their daffodils in April and took home the dark red fragrance of their peonies in June—they might someday be glad their plants hadn't exhausted themselves going to seed. While we read in the evening, we breathed in these clear scents and waited for the peonies to drop all their petals at once in a gorgeous silken ring around the vase. Marie said it was Chinese artifice to make a natural flower the color and texture of fabric and cause all the bright color to fall in one completed gesture.

But the place seemed to be unobtainable, until we heard the sawing and hammering of roof repair one fall day. So all its tadpoles and mosquitoes now belonged to somebody. And somebody tried to make a vegetable garden there too in that rocky soil. We saw fencing near the road where I couldn't recall any place for a garden. Too much work kept me from baking a loaf of bread to give the new neighbors a proper welcome, but one summer day I turned to walk into the empty driveway in the old way on an impulse to find the garden. Little was changed in the yard. Above the flowering quince a little bed of strawberries had been tucked in. I noted that its netting was held up by hoops bent from a tough old vine and found my way to the garden.

Everything about it was simple and ingenious. It was obviously a man's garden because it had involved heavy construction. Not that a man wouldn't undertake labors like that for a woman, but you really can't do that sort of thing for someone else, to order. Its maker imagined it as he was making it, developed it out of its place and even out of the clearing of the place. It was all one gesture, from fencing to planting. He'd found the stone foundation of an old house by the road, taken the trash, rank trees, and creeper vines out of it, half filled it with soil, and let it face south. He'd fenced it high with chicken wire, the posts and framing from trees he'd cleared. Some rails rested on forked limbs, some were lashed to the uprights with vines. Every corner was different, and there was hardly a nail in the thing. Nothing ramshackle about it, it was thrifty and shipshape like the work of a sailor.

He'd got the garden started good and early. Beans were climbing up the side walls, cucumbers were setting fruit, tomato plants looked stout, and the kohlrabi were glorious. Rows were true and clean, paths indicated by stones turned up during excavation. There were some plants I'd never seen before, which tickled me, but also quite a few potatoes and all the necessary herbs. It was the garden of a cook. Already the broccoli was getting away from him, as it always does.

I remember in England being shown his garden with a hospitable courtesy by the father of one of my children's friends. Everything about England was new to me, but I recognized at Kew that I was seeing gardens the like of which I would never see in any other land. This gardener showed me gooseberries larger than I thought possible. His garden seemed small, but as we went round, I realized it might have been a shell or a maze, so much more was there, so inward and surprising were the turns, the new openings and pleasures. Later as I told his daughter how beautiful I had thought it, I mentioned that though I was merely acquainted with her father, I thought he must be like his garden—more than he might seem if you weren't paying attention. She looked startled a moment, but—perhaps her father's daughter, beautiful and reserved as his garden—said nothing.

Nor should she, because a garden is not interpretable. It's a finding and untranslatable, like a poem that says itself if you can listen. We can't tell from a garden whether the gardener has sown pain or blitheness in it—or both. We go sometimes from the worst news of people brutalizing each other into our gardens, not to escape the truth, but to have a space to think it out more patiently.

I spotted a frog in my neighbor's garden as I left it. He gleamed his golden side at me as he leaped away. On the way out I caught sight of a crooked basket woven of branches and vines, a jeu d'esprit, for it was too open to hold anything. It was made in an interval of work, probably, for it had to have been plaited when vines were pliable and branches green. The unthinkable labor of clearing out an old foundation when you haven't the funds to order it done for you had thrown up a grin along the way. I thought that our new neighbors had already enjoyed their daffodils and peonies, but probably hadn't yet found the gooseberries, almost imperishable, wild and small, but the first free fruits of summer after all.

19 : *Prolific and Devourer*

When we found this house twenty-three years ago, an old pear tree clung to the ridge behind the kitchen. There were the usual lot of fruit trees, of course: summer and fall apples, plum, peach, and another pear all off at a distance from the house. Some, like the apples, were a good sixty years old, music from another age. The kitchen pear looked ancient, a mere crescent at ground level, its pith so gone you could see daylight through the shell in one or two spots. Clearly it wasn't going to last long, and Leonard planted a pine southeast of it, over my objections to anticipations that block light.

The given sometimes poses problems for the receiver. One is abundance. The prolific, says Blake, needs the devourer "to receive the excess of his delights." Of course soft fruits like peaches are easy to eat immediately. The plum was unpredictable for anything but mold, and the distant pear had eccentric ideas about setting fruit. But one youthful apple tree bore delicious, tart fruit freely, and we had a hard time keeping up with it in the fall when everything else was calling out for harvest and preservation. I didn't begin by liking pears especially, but it would be churlish to refuse an offering.

In fact I got fond of its gallantry, the panache of its blossoms in spring just outside the humdrum, kitcheny round of my own days. I liked it best in August when the birds are sadly silent, molting, and insect sounds take over. If I had to have such a simple ground, a mere drone, then let me have a lively treble over it, a pavan and a galliard, as in Elizabethan lute duets. I couldn't get it in sound, of course, for the pear tree was no lute, though lutes are pear-shaped. But I was entertained by the tree's yearly variations on its theme of "Pear." Prudently it dropped most of its early set of fruit in June. Then in August, while the katydids kept up their tiresome argument about whether she did or she didn't, the pear swelled and ripened only the perfect number, to show its full range from the highest fret to the lowest string: six or seven pears.

Still it couldn't last long. Meanwhile the summer apples aged, the tart young apple tree toppled over on a windless day, the peaches reached term and withered to the root. And insect-eating birds were very busy in the pear, not a good sign, though at least a balance was at work.

But then all the devourers are feverish in the heat of high summer. The borer seems to get my summer squashes almost as soon as they sprout, and as they decline, still blossoming, shield bugs move in to finish them off. Beetles lace our favorite bean plants. The catbird visits my late-fruiting blueberry early every morning, thrashes his tail, and yells at me and my cat in my garden. We all suffer. My son-in-law, the chef, calls me to report that during his one-week absence a woodchuck set up house in the middle of his tomato patch and takes one bite out of each good tomato every night. I don't know whether he's more outraged at the location of the den or at the beast's finicky eating habits.

The endurance of the pear suggests that getting devourers to devour each other would be a good idea all around, but there's more symmetry in art than in nature, unfortunately. Or perhaps not, since even the order of art is beyond the power of one brain to take it in. I love to read about change ringing because forms like the "treble bob" are part of the Renaissance love of a pattern so energetically elaborate (as in knot gardens or sestinas) as to break out of fixity, causing space to move and sound to have spatial presence. A sestina feels like a dance as the end words move and change places, very much like "plain hunting" in change ringing, in which all the bells work regularly from first place, or *lead* (the treble), to last, or *behind* (the tenor), a movement called "hunting up"—and back again, called "hunting or coursing down."

Change ringing can be even more dancelike or full of action, as the metaphor from hunting implies, for one bell in a set may have a plain hunt while another bell goes only so far before it strikes twice and then goes back, causing the other bells to "dodge," or step backwards in their course up or down. In certain modifications of the coursing order some bells double dodge.

And if the mind isn't already boggled, the number of possible changes for any given set of bells increases exponentially with the number of bells. So three bells give $1 \times 2 \times 3 = 6$ changes, four bells, $6 \times 4 = 24$ changes, five bells give $24 \times 5 = 120$ changes, and seven bells, 5,040 changes, the standard number for a peal. I can barely imagine the time and strength it takes seven men to ring a peal. Bunyan accuses his "much delight in ringing" as "vain," but it was certainly not harum-scarum. Perhaps bell ringing, even if it is vanity, tempts an intelligent man because it is mindful and energetic.

So bell ringers, ordinary village men, hunt their courses, poets write crowns of sonnets and very long poems in ottava rima, mothers orchestrate families of divergent personalities, gardeners juggle weather, soil, space, color, and texture. The lute writers do something like change ringing also, with pieces like "Twenty Waies upon the Bells" and "The New Hunt Is Up." And in a favorite, witty Renaissance metaphor of music-making and sexuality, John Dowland writes a duet for "two to playe upon one lute." All these persons move like dancers, neither through fixed space or changing air, but in the body's imagined knowledge.

Unluckily in this year of abundant rain the pear tree lost its head in the production of dozens of pears. And in August a ridge wind took off that airy treble with all its burgeoning fruit. It's not through yet, however. I see that one lower branch has been heading up and may make a leader, if Perry's genius can trim the old bole, arranging a kind of double dodge. The new leader even sports one golden ripe pear. Maybe pears live to great age. I recall that "lute" comes from the Arabic *al'ud,* "the piece of wood," and think that if I'm lucky, my well-seasoned lute may stay with me yet a while.

20 : *Michaelmas*

All tasks are part of an idea, and if you're lucky enough to be free, they're part of your own idea. A friend tells me that she associates gardening with picking beans as a child in midday heat, but that sounds more like farm labor to me. Once I was witless enough to grow lots of onions, but when I had to hoe the rows in good daylight, I recovered my right mind. On the other hand my friend loves nothing better than to manage house construction. I can see the charm of this until it comes to the shopping, the boredom of which to me is almost toxic.

In your own task, you hardly notice the work, even when it's hard labor, because it's materializing your idea so urgently. There are maintenance chores, of course, which might seem boring, but in high summer when the sun doesn't set till nine, chores seem to make your idea shine, and you hold on to one more day of the days allotted you, stretching it out in work and answering for it to your credit. But by this day, the twenty-ninth of September, the feast of Michaelmas, the urgency of that attachment between work and idea loosens.

Today calls up the image of its namesake angel, a figure of power in so many Renaissance paintings. Just as the sociable Raphael is always accompanied by Tobias's little dog, the warrior Michael is always recognizable by his armor. But he was also a figure of judgment. In many paintings he holds a balance, one pan containing a small infant, which is the anima or psyche of the person who is pictured waiting anxiously at Michael's feet to see whether his life has been sufficient. I think of the archangel when days and nights balance and seem to stay even for a time as the season turns.

You can feel the tension of the balance now when the sun rises and sets pretty much true east and west. You think that however much risings and settings stray in solstice time, at the equinox the truth of east and west is going to pull you into line. The geese have been gathering for weeks, settling down in the evenings with loud callings on the flatlands by the creek below. But now they rise at sunrise and depart. Raucous, disordered, insistent, their cries to each other make you wonder why you stop everything to listen to them. But as they rise above the ridge this morning, the land seems to lift with them for a moment, along with some muscle in your chest. You feel a surge of inner life in the land, a shudder or anima about to pull it straight to its four corners.

A good tool has something like the same effect on its worker. We don't notice it in simple tools like trowels, and we're cut off from it altogether in power tools. But the first time you use a scythe, figuring out where your double grasp goes, hefting and swinging it, you realize that the tool is teaching you to work, that the work has been designed into it and emerges through your learning body. The reach of the scythe—and all tools are levers—stretches you toward your rising or setting and balances you on the stretch.

Summer garden jobs please me because they're linked to each other in an order orderly enough to make sense out of them all, yet not in an iron chain on my time. I can loosen a link to fit an evening in between—or a week, a month, a season. This summer I got hay to mulch the old, worn-out asparagus bed, but first I planned to fill its empty spaces with multiplied daylilies, which I must move to find spots for the increasing iris, moving which—if I can find the right other place for the achillea—will clear the neglected end of the former storage bed for future tomatoes. I haven't got past the iris stage yet, however.

From my study window I look down on the chaos of an idea about an herb garden near the kitchen door. When parsley faded here but flourished at the end of the tomato bed, I realized my idea had changed its mind and its location too. Now the materiality of the herb garden is left, without its idea, most of it taken over by tough rue and seedy savory. Chaos is hard to keep your eye on because you can't see where one idea has strayed into another. There's also a little crowd of mints here. When I saw them running rampant in a neighbor's garden, I put them here where I could keep an eye on them. And I see they look beautiful: the blue-purple bottle brushes of the anise hyssop thrust up into the light above the winy, ruffled perilla, hazed by a crowd of sleepy bees.

I think about this as I idle in the garden, letting today's diamond air sparkle on my head and shoulders, eyeing the seeding crabgrass. But mostly I look at the ranked horizons of the whole south meadow: the sun on the tossing ridge locusts, the dogwood below—still and unshining as it purples its leaves—and lower, the vervain, wildly branching its flowers into the sun above the garden fence to shine lavender back at you, vivid at midday and more vivid still holding the last of the sunset light.

I wonder what makes any order out of this—or an order apparent enough to please in the garden where I work out my love of order against my aversion to managing or being managed. I check out the red onion I left hanging on the fence last fall that dropped to grow its own onion community out of my way, without my assistance, pursuing its apparently seamless cycle so that I don't know when to break into it to harvest serviceable red onions. I admire its new green shoots, and it says, *"Non serviam."*

But probably the order is inner, like the one Asa Gray analyzes in his *Botany,* in the section on phyllotaxy, "the position and order of leaves upon the stem." He celebrates symmetrical order, "every leaf governed by a simple arithmetical law, which fixes beforehand the precise place it is to occupy upon the stem." Alternate leaves of apple trees, for example, arranged in five ranks, spiral around the stem twice before the sixth leaf appears directly above the first. The system is expressed by the fraction $\frac{2}{5}$, two being the number of turns around the stem completing one set of leaves, and five the number of leaves in each cycle, or the number of perpendicular ranks.

It's perfectly simple, the series of fractions for different ranks being $\frac{1}{2}$, $\frac{1}{3}$, $\frac{2}{5}$, $\frac{3}{8}$, $\frac{5}{13}$, $\frac{8}{21}$, and so on. And an elegant series, "the numerator and denominator of each fraction being those of the next two preceding ones added together"—a Fibonacci series, in fact, though Gray doesn't burden his scholars with such pedantry. It's all alive in Gray's sense of it, "according as the formative energy in its spiral course up the developing stem lays down at corresponding intervals 2, 3, 5, 13, or 21 ranks of alternate leaves."

The same order lies in the flower buds, for flowers, as it turns out, "are altered branches, and their parts, therefore, altered leaves." The petals of the rose, then (the apple being a member of the larger Rose family), must be folded in the bud in the spiraling, five-ranked order of its cousin. Though I could never have analyzed this order, I feel the formative energy of its spiraling upward course—and maybe I can sense its linking power.

The inner order of every plant must in some way be visible or apparent, must organize the large order beyond me of the ridge trees and link that with the small order of my garden, subsuming its incidental disorders. As I lay hands on them, the plants are probably stretching through me to teach me their work. Raphael's greeting was, "Joy be to thee always." And I might hear a whisper like that if I make it past the day of Michael.

21 : *Metabolism*

Cold air is pouring over the country, but the earth is still warm from the long summer. It's the season of worms. They are under the mulch everywhere, almost on top of the soil, and have made a layer of castings over the beds. As I dig, I go through their knobby soil and push my small bulbs down into earth warmer than the air. Frost nips in two or three times a week and gradually takes the tenderest plants, leaving the tough ones like calendula, which looks soft as any of its departed neighbors. Yet, John Gerard tells us, the calendula "floureth from Aprill or May even untill Winter, and in Winter also, if it bee warm."

The trees grow lighter. Even on an overcast day the maples seem to shine flame and yellow into the windows on the dark side of the house. Along the roads you can once more see through to the land beyond the bordering trees. Streams start to trickle in the beds you forgot were there and under stone walls through the little square openings curiously built into them eighty-four years ago by persons whose business it was to engineer pipelines, but also to know stone walls, the paths of the kills, and all their little tributaries. The cold starts the streams; cold is their running sign. You look into their cidery shallows and see minnows so small they could sleep in drops. You wonder how they can endure the winter, but they must find unfreezing beds in the Esopus when they all tumble down there. The land sheds its water as the trees their leaves.

I poke through the old books I have picked up at some library fair, especially the cookbooks, for our metabolism seems to change when the season changes. We think about plants in winter in consuming ways, because we need them for the chemical changes in our cells that provide energy for life and repair of waste. I have to be careful turning the books' leaves so as not to lose the four-leaf clovers that their former owners tucked in—perhaps at some favorite pickle recipe—and wonder whether the clover leaves issued forth in 1901 or 1918 along with the book leaves. I like the idea of "spider corn bread" or "graham gems"—though I'm not sure what "gems" are. I find, however, that I've lent my spider to my son John, having urged on him the information that the pan imparts its iron to whatever you cook in it. So I settle down to the big dictionary and the wonderful sounds of "anabolism" and "catabolism."

These terms define our unbreakable links to the plants, we being conspicuously catabolic: decomposing and oxidizing protoplasm into something simpler with a liberation of energy. Telling words, "liberation" and "energy." And we owe our liberation and our energy to the plants, whose anabolism builds up substances into more complex living protoplasm. We require complex organic substances like protein and carbohydrates, and we break them up and excrete simple substances. We are analytic beings.

Of course metabolism is the sum of both these processes, and if we were liberated enough we'd probably feel somewhat more anabolic among the plants: as though we too could build up, and with an economy of energy. We do this in mind-work, of course, and the great minders of human life seem to work with an almost vegetative ease. Everyone experiences it in dreaming. Susanne Langer remarks that dreaming is so fundamental to humans that it goes on without effort, like metabolism. As with breathing, it's easier to dream than not to dream. And a good deal of dreaming goes on among the plants in one way or another.

I pick up Asa Gray's *School and Field Book of Botany,* which I bought for twenty-five cents in 1987. It's inscribed "Adella R. Goodrich, May 26, 1887." I can hardly realize that I hold in my hand and use a book over one hundred years old. At first I thought it may have been bought for a season of gardening or field tripping, but truth to tell, it looks unread. So I imagine it as a school prize for excellence in studies and Miss Goodrich as a young lady too full of juice to spend the summer botanizing.

Gray's publisher introduces him by noting that he begins with "*first principles*" and progresses "by easy stages until the student, who is at all diligent, is enabled to master the intricacies of the science." Few writers know first principles and the easy stages that issue out of them. Gray knows them, and he must have been an extraordinary teacher. I take the greatest pleasure in his masterful analysis, which has made sense of what I thought I knew and carried me beyond it. He gives no information piecemeal, but foreknows every part's perfection in a whole through which he moves with the exuberant patience of easy genius. Stepping carefully in his footsteps, I could teach a six or seven year old the beginnings of botany.

John Gerard begins his *Herball* with an "Epistle Dedicatorie" to his patron, the noble William Cecil, whose honors, taking six lines to list, end in the resounding, "Lord high Treasurer of *England*." Cecil's garden, I take it, was at Hatfield House, which Cecil was given, like it or not, in exchange by Henry Tudor, who had an awkward habit of purloining manors he desired. It was an age when a mere man of knowledge did well to place himself near a man of power, at least of more worldly power than himself.

Gerard praises plants especially for their "hidden vertue"—such that the "very bruit beasts have found it out." "Hidden vertue" is a good description of anabolism, the plants' interior power of synthesis. He cannot, of course, define it analytically because he has no powerful abstractions or scientific terms, but his writing is filled with its energy. In gathering his *Herball*, Gerard (I understand) followed rather too closely in another man's footsteps, but what must be his own are the incomparably vigorous and accurate descriptions of common plants, or a rare one of which he will note, "It groweth in my garden." When you read him, you realize that you've looked at plants but never really seen them, as witness this remarkable passage of observation:

> The Cucumber creepes alongst upon the ground all about, with long rough branches; whereupon doe grow rough leaves uneven about the edges: from the bosome whereof come forth crooked clasping tendrils like those of the Vine. The floures shoot forth betweene the stalkes and the leaves, set upon tender foot-stalkes composed of five small yellow leaves: which being past, the fruit succeedeth, long, cornered, rough, and set with certaine bumpes or risings, greene at the first, and yellow when they be ripe, wherein is contained a firme and sollid pulpe or substance transparent or thorow-shining, which together with the seed is eaten a little before they be fully ripe. The seeds be white, long, and flat.

This is perfectly accurate and all alive. The plant seems to spring up from its creeping along the ground and grow through all its stages before your eyes in one remarkable sentence. But it is not yet scientific description. There is one touch of counting—five flower parts—but Gerard has apparently no concept of "petal." He says "yellow leaves." The whole thing in the beautiful concrete language of sense is close to literature. In fact it's a model for contemporary writers in the easy power of its verbs.

Gerard used his plants for healing, and I'm surprised that what he says, for example, of woundwort from his own experience hasn't prompted investigation such as scientists undertake in remote rain forests. Of course they might have been put off by his description elsewhere—somewhat ambiguously witnessed—of geese developing out of a "barnacle tree," though he suggests that he records this "raritie" mainly for the "honor" of England. The dream of honor is hard to resist. Gerard has heard a whisper of detachment, however. He draws back from a more refined history of the "barnacle tree" because, he says, that requires "a deeper search into the bowels of Nature, than my intended purpose will suffer me to wade into, my sufficiencie also considered." This is the worm wiggling off the hook. But he certainly knows how to grow tropical plants in temperate climes, and if I had followed his advice, my cucumber might not have quit by August. I might have gathered its thorow-shining till frost and say, though more modestly than he, "It groweth in my garden."

Amidst its sensuous concreteness and even with no scientific terms at hand, Gerard's language is testably accurate. Gray, for his part, is too good a teacher not to know that technical terms can be the death of discourse, especially when your purpose is no less than a wading into the bowels of Nature. Gray uses scientific terms easily in his own supple language. Here is what he says about organic beings: each individual is "formed of inorganic or mineral matter, that is, of earth and air, indeed; but only . . . under the influence of life: and after life departs, sooner or later, it is decomposed into earth and air again." I can see that I work in that earth and air today.

Gerard and Gray are like two halves of a kind of metabolism of mind, one building up (though sometimes in curious castings) nutritive substances for thought; the other analytic, breaking down the protoplasm of the subject into simpler bodies for understanding. And I for my part—my sufficiencie also considered—am lucky in my books, my worms, and my ninety-year-old four-leaf clovers, still snug and green in the warm pages of their book. I found in my dictionary that a "gem" is "a muffin made of coarse flour and sometimes unleavened," which sounds hearty and simple enough for dinner on a frosty night.

22 : *Spectating*

Perry Cobb is working on the area on the dark, northwest side of our house, the walls of which we extended out eight feet last fall and crammed with windows. The extension changed what was a dim corridor into a living room and lets in light. We had never paid much attention to the land on this side of the house before we had an outlook on it. But now that there are windows to the floor, we thought we'd like to look at something more sightly than rocks thrown up by construction or a slope whose centerpiece is a shabby old well house covered with green roll roofing. Improvement probably meant grading and building walks and steps. I thought of someone else doing all the hard stuff, after which I would fill in the delightful empty places with shade-loving flowers and the extra perennials that multiply around the garden and that I can't throw away. The project would be simple, green, and thrifty.

I began to imagine the steps. I have long seen pictures of many beautiful garden steps. I thought about their lovely curves, the ferny or feathery leaf patterns of the plants embowering their sides, the sweet bulbs in the spring, the easy naturalness of it all, and especially the way steps bind a spell onto a place. I have always passionately wanted garden steps. So I caught Perry one day when he intermitted the perpetual flight of his yellow truck to say hello.

As we chatted about our summer routines, I began to see that he works continuously, and the light faded from my notion of hiring him. We talked about vegetable gardens and food, and I saw that he eats like a true ectomorph, tiny meals every few hours, nothing heavy to nauseate his delicate stomach, and much of it on the sugar side of carbohydrates. Grinning, he told me that he relies on sweets for the quick energy he needs for work. My first instinct was dismay, but then it's best to reserve judgment when you face an idea in full function.

I asked him when he got a chance to work in his own garden or his nursery, since he's on his jobs till nine in the evening. "Oh, I work there after supper till eleven or so." "By floodlight?" I said, but he laughed and shrugged off artificial lights, saying he knows where everything is, and besides, "there's light." I decided not to pursue the optics of the natural light of summer nights, for I already have enough suspicions that we all of us live in different worlds. The image of Perry digging happily in his nursery at eleven-thirty at night after a twelve-hour working day reminded me forcibly that what looks like torment and insanity to some, as Blake says, is to others a walking among the fires of genius, delighting in its enjoyments.

When I mentioned my project, he went right over to look at the space, developing ideas as he paced about. He studied the empty place under the huge pine that I had been content to ignore because nothing except the suckers of an ancient lilac will grow in dense evergreen shade. I was surprised to hear the words "viburnum," "andromeda," "cotoneaster," and "hemlock." With plenty of experience of shade-gardening in the city, I had read every book in the library on the subject and found that most garden "writers" are really recirculators, repeating some earlier "authority" and don't know what they're talking about in hard cases. Doubtless a yew will grow in shade, but who wants a skinny, pathetic thing, yellow without light, its roots gasping in the desert soil that is half the problem with shade. And our well is extremely slow; I can't water for more than twenty minutes.

But Perry whipped his clippers out of his pocket, beheaded the saplings of slippery elm and hickory reaching for the light, and applied his scuffle hoe to a bad grade to get a better feel of it. "Isn't it a little shady under this big pine tree for a pieris?" I ventured. "Well," said he, "I kind of like the way the pine branches reach way over to the road. Of course, the pieris might not *bloom*." So I let the question go, not wanting to appear demanding. The sight of the well house, he said, could be blocked with a weeping yew. I wondered about the deer, which don't seem to find yew poisonous, but in the face of all Perry's experience I didn't say anything. He left, saying he could work me in.

He came two or three times in the summer, putting in railway ties to divide the grade into beds and laying down gravel to begin paths. I wanted to brighten up the new beds with Impatiens or work some of the long-time tenants out of the storage bed, but there seemed to be too much construction going on. I was at a stand, a mere spectator, unable to see into someone else's imagination. No one mentioned steps.

I enjoyed watching Perry's sinewy efficiency, however. The yellow truck would arrive, and before I could get out to greet him, he and his helper would be shoving a tie into place or wheelbarrowing gravel up the slope. One day he arrived with drains to be ditched under the eaves, and it developed that a piece of thick old sidewalk, about three and a half feet square, was going to be moved into position as a stepping-off platform for the porch steps. And it was moved, though it appeared to have cemented itself to a large rock underneath and to weigh, all told, about eight hundred pounds. It was levered up, its underlying rock balanced on boards, and rolled along with many stops on three lengths of plumbing pipe. I felt I was witnessing a moving of the Sphinx and got out my camera to record the event.

Naturally that was all for a while—except for one tie emplaced as a step in the middle of the grade—and I figured the project was over for the season, what with October drawing to a close. Then the other evening Perry and his helper arrived about six-thirty. When I got outside, he had unloaded seven small shrubs and cut three or four long branches out of the pine, "to let in a little sun here and there," he said, gesturing toward the darkening sky.

He and his helper shoved in a tie for another step; then Perry considered the lighting of the new path. I admitted that Leonard usually assists guests down to their cars with a flashlight, especially when the grade is slippery with pine needles. We've often regretted that the porch floodlight doesn't illuminate the old stone steps going down to the road. With a gesture Perry described one light shining on the path and one up into the pine. I could envision that. Many's the night after guests have left in the rain, we've hung out on the porch just to look under the red leaves of the Japanese maple at the pine boughs with a thousand drops along their needles, shining, shining every which way in the floodlight.

Perry complained of a sore palm where he'd driven a thorn deep into it. I advised a good twenty-minute soaking to work it out, but as I held his hand to read the palm, I couldn't see any such leisure in its future. He smiled into the empty place under the pine, now ringed with shrubs in pots. "In summer you can bring your hose in here and just wet it down for half an hour or so." He took another look at the place and stepped back. "Some-

thing like a bird feeder in the middle, and I'm going to bring a rock in."
The feeder rattled me, but I could see the idea of a rock. I pointed out that
rocks were hanging around all over the place, including those in an old
stone wall across the road. "Oh, I don't mean a *stone-wall* rock," he said. I
was immediately ashamed of my small-mindedness. "I mean a *big* rock."

Now I was back in the dark, wondering what diameter of pipe would
facilitate the moving of a *big* rock. I turned on the floodlight for the helper,
who was filling in dirt behind the new step. At eight o'clock he and Perry
packed up their tools and departed in the yellow truck down the road in
what you might call deep dusk.

Year Four

23 : *Feasting and Preserving*

The rule of the vegetable garden is, Feast as much as possible, and then preserve. An almost antithetical rule, for feasting springs out of the temporal prodigality of the season, while preserving tries to make the temporary substantial enough to keep. To know a vegetable, you use it up, eat it in its prime because it's not simply best then, it's only itself then. The long green things you see in the store are not recognizable as the nutty, delicately sweet asparagus you can cut, cook, and serve within fifteen minutes. You can eat the store things, of course, and benefit, but there's none of the delicious hilarity of unique identity, the fun of the inexhaustible character of a thing that is itself only.

The beautiful fullness of coming into season leads to feasting, but then to preserving because production doesn't stop with the prime in beans and cucumbers and overwhelms even feasting in tomatoes. When we were children, preserving was prodigal but unconnected to feasting on your own vegetables, for only country people had vegetable gardens. We were like Puritans, cut off from the paganness of the garden—and with its fruits, only industrious.

My mother was no Puritan, however. In the midst of our steamy labor of pitting endless cherries, stoning apricots, skinning tomatoes, pears, and peaches, stringing and snapping beans, cutting corn off the cob, chopping onions and celery, jamming strawberries, and jellying currants, she would show me her hands and ask me to recognize that they were the hands of a woman made for better things than rounds of hard work. I wasn't quite sure what the signs of a higher calling were, but, pretty deep in slimy peach skins myself, I hoped my future didn't include a canning cellar. Still the full jars looked beautiful with their glowing colors, and—rank on rank on cellar shelves—they proclaimed variety, the parsimony of thrift banished by extravagant energy and appetite. Winter dinners of roast pork were sumptuous with pickled peaches or spicy crab apples.

Perhaps there's a tendency to excess in even modest feasting. In the country we honor the asparagus by serving it first as its own course, and once guests who'd never had real asparagus fell upon it so determinedly that I nipped off down to the asparagus bed to cut another platterful while they were finishing the first. Another time a guest, jaded with official cooking, perhaps, ate only the very tips of her asparagus, to the fascinated horror of other guests who were trying to keep their wits on the conversation and their eyes off her plate. A friend confessed later that she was trying to think of a graceful way of confiscating the stems, but the woman's husband, acting either in his capacity of asparagus lover or diplomat, reached over casually and took those tender stems.

As if cultivated feasting weren't enough, we used to go out to gather wild black caps in season, swathed in long garments and mosquito repellent. This was cheerful, and the children in the twilight started to sing "Row, Row Your Boat." But we were interrupted by an indignant cardinal, who threw himself into the topmost branch of an elm and whipped out a torrent of crystalline whistles. It was late in the day for him to sing, but he had evidently found us—in his territory—intolerable amateurs.

And probably music is a better feast than food. One morning in September, the cricket in the kitchen began to sing not in cricket creaks but reedy gurgles, a whole loud trill, rather like a bird, stirred perhaps by the ravishing passage from *The Magic Flute* he was listening to from his perch atop the door frame, black against the white wall, antennae forward and alert. His sweet warble was a sugar produced to preserve the abundant temporality of Mozart through the quiet winter of the house.

His ardent attention reminded me of our evening at Molly's with her music group. Nothing but a feast of music could exceed one of Molly's dinners. And this was not a dinner but a chance to sit like quiet crickets listening to singers and instrumentalists come together in one group or another as the freedom of the day and the music they brought with them moved them to sing and play. Late at night only my friend Bette and I were left as guests and only two musicians were still awake. One of them drew out a new piece of music, and Molly picked up someone's tenor recorder. Though neither had seen or heard the piece before, they went at it perfectly, as I knew because I happened to have a recording of it. When the owner of the recorder turned up and took his instrument, the piece went on with Molly la-la-ing the continuo.

When the last drop of music had fallen, Bette and I walked gently down the streamy road, giddy with counterpoint and moonlight. We preserved, though creakily, the energy of the evening and our appetite for music by lifting our voices in a few rounds of "Row, Row Your Boat."

We'd never dream of trying to preserve asparagus, gone when it is gone, not to come again for another year. But in the fall, dwarf horticultural beans can be shelled and kept or celebrated in the most genial of feasts, succotash, as Leonard's parents and grandparents going way back prepared it in southern Indiana. They probably had quite fresh sweet corn, sweet onion, and maybe even beefsteak tomatoes as glorious as our Belgian Giants. But it's partly the mixture of guests who've never eaten succotash before and old friends waiting, knives in hand, for the towel to come off the platter of hot corn on the cob that develops a mild hilarity as the dinner goes on.

Newcomers may be politely puzzled. It all looks very plain, set forth in bowls and platters. Besides the corn, there are dwarf horticultural beans, floating brownly in their juices, raw chopped sweet onion, and platters of freshly sliced, rosy tomatoes, some salt, and perhaps a bit of butter if anyone wants it. No garlic, no spices or sauces, nothing to make a restaurant dish, if you have a French restaurant in mind. Leonard, who has grown, shelled, and cooked the beans, gives the only advice: "Cut your corn into your bowl—and be sure to scrape the milk kernels off the cob. Then add everything else to taste."

As good as the melange of food is the mixture of guests. Some pile their first helpings perilously high by the time they've adjusted proportions. When they finally get it right, they can't eat in peace because their neighbors are asking them to pass more onions or tomatoes or beans. The conversation bubbles into laughter, but some guests, I notice, gaze steadfastly into their bowls, deeply considering, and finally offer general theories about proportion and which is the *main* ingredient, which are hailed by half the table and hooted down by the other half. Like the food, the guests, though well mixed, retain each an own identity.

It's one kind of American feast, not just because it's regional, but because in purity and freshness it's part of the privilege of American plenty. Then as the harvest catches up with us, we find ingenious ways to preserve simply—no canning. (And the last tall, bright jar had gone from the cellar shelves by the time I cleared out my mother's house.) And yet, in the clear, we can't resist the last bit of wild fruit. I gather quinces. Bette decides to make jelly and borrows the old canner I found in the house and have of course not thrown away. She quarters and boils quinces, lets the last drop fall from the jelly bag, and adds the sugar and slow fire that will change it all into the sweet, tart, amber-brandy essence of the summer past. Honey to the corn milk, it will remind us of paradise.

We begin at the center, and if we go out from it, we must return from time to time or create it elsewhere as a new center. This is particularly interesting in the United States, where most of us are immigrants. Even Native Americans have been harried from the places where we found them and displaced further by the name "Indians." But native cultures have their own wandering and seeking traditions, as expressed in the Hopi narratives of coming into the fourth world. In the gray third world, they say, the beginning people wondered, "Where can we go? Is there another place?" But they didn't know of another place and were troubled until an old man said, "Have we not heard footsteps in the sky, as though someone is walking there?"

Once you have asked this question, it's only a step to creating messengers and singing them up into the sky to investigate things. I think about some of this on a soft October day in Branchville, Indiana. Leonard has come to see his kinsman, Mansfield Frakes, who has kept an eye on the timberland Leonard and his sister still own here in Perry County, where they spent summers as children visiting their grandparents. We are in the graveyard at the top of a high hill looking at gravestones with deeply familiar names. From the hill we can see the timberland across the sparkle of the branch, a stream running into the Ohio, which is about five miles away with Kentucky on its far side.

There are more families here than are left in Branchville, consisting now of a center of about five houses and a church. The gravestones are history and testimony. Old worn limestone discourses with polished granite, and Leonard's grandparents have both an old stone and a newer granite one saying that Sarepta and Thomas Jefferson Deen lie here, beloved parents. Many sad stories. Martha Sprinkle seems to have lost several infants, one for whom a single date tells his life: January 2, 1885. One tall old limestone says only, "Our Baby."

I look for the stone of Stephen Bovinet (September 11, 1866–May 27, 1912), for I had heard a comment on the inscription for a man who killed his wife with an ax and then shot himself after telling his five-year-old son to step outside. Sure enough, the stone says, "Asleep in Jesus." Leonard's father suggested another place for him, but I think the phrase says something about how in a community the whole context of an act is known and so the act is forgiven. Of course it also says that it is more conventional to forgive violence to women and children. Inscriptions seem to close these narratives, but time opens them.

Leonard's uncle Leroy is here, the one who got the farm half of the original land grant but suffered a strangulated hernia, too far from a hospital to survive it. His wife, with young children, couldn't carry on the farming of over a hundred acres by herself and sold the place. I don't find the grave of Arthur, Sarepta's oldest son, who got a Ph.D. in history and didn't have much "common sense," Nellie Frakes says. By that she may mean his escapade of marrying, at age sixty, a seventeen-year-old girl. Or she may be thinking of his manifest incapacity right from the start for any of the practical tasks like fence repair that make farming on hard land possible. He is said to have bought a car when cars were new things and, unable to repair its first flat, had it put up on blocks in the barn, where it may be still.

Leonard's father, too, had no knack for things like grubbing out stumps and followed his brother's lead away and got a Ph.D. in American literature. This is a well-recognized pattern in American culture, the leap from farm to university; one of Thomas's brothers had become a medical doctor. And I have always noticed that those with no psychological aptitude for a practical task display an obvious physical clumsiness in its performance that excuses them from being asked to do it again. They know nothing about fence posts, but they have money in the bank and put up good-naturedly with terms like "no common sense."

The large trees have disappeared from the top of a nearby hill where Thomas and Sarepta housed children and an odd relative or two in a double log cabin, the cabin now replaced by a brick house. The tall old walnut trees around the house and a huge hickory have been swept away by storms. There used to be a road along the branch that went switchback up to the house. By the branch Thomas had a workshop where in any spare time he hewed oak into railroad ties and made yokes for cattle and sheep. "You don't hardly see sheep with yokes," says Mansfield, and I look closely at him, because I have noticed his formidable powers of language and irony. "But that was for roguish sheep," he adds. Thomas certainly lived under the yoke, hiring himself and his team out to clear land, which meant the backbreaking labor of hauling out stumps. The life of the house, Leonard says, was on this side: the workshop, the well, and the branch with a swimming hole in it, access to them now gone or grown over.

I ask Mansfield to say his relation to Leonard, which he does patiently: his grandfather, Grayson Frakes, was a brother of John Frakes, father of Sarepta, and they married sisters. But just a touch of genealogy reveals that everyone is doubly related. Mansfield is a powerful man, the genius of the place. He could never leave. His house next to the church, his book a worn copy of the *History of Perry County*, and his head full of observations and narratives, he's the embodiment of the scientific, humane, and literary learning of his cousins. His narratives are rich, pungent, and apparently local, but I was startled to hear one story that, with geographical changes, was straight out of Boccaccio. The local runs deeper than we imagine.

In the Oriole graveyard, a couple of miles away, we visit the Walkers, Leonard's mother's side of the family. And here poor Leonard breaks down at the grave of Roy Walker, his mother's cousin, who took Leonard squirrel shooting, fishing, fence mending in the summer. He could do anything. If a squirrel got down in a hollow tree, Roy took a bit of green briar and twisted it into the hole to catch the squirrel out by the tail. He had come home from the First World War with bad lungs, but enabled Avanell Walker (Leonard's grandmother), the mother of six children, to farm in the absence of her husband, an absence accounted for by its own cycle of narratives, probably. A violent temper? Epilepsy? He was not to be yoked down in Oriole, at any rate. At the farm, the well is gone and the barn where Leonard used to read in the wheat bin.

If Mansfield is the *locus genii*, Nell is the muse of the place. Though she can cook a magnificent dinner for distant kin (squirrel, dumplings in gravy, green beans well cooked with bacon, biscuits, cauliflower in vinegar, pickles, sliced tomato, corn, and squash pie with whipped cream—all from home supply) and makes her own towels and sheets, she doesn't care for house affairs. She's skilled in arts, from the making of shadow memorial boxes to her great love, music, and teaches piano to children all about. I'm enthralled by her beautiful high forehead. She tells me about her only child, Edward, named after her favorite brother who had died at twenty-four of complications from measles, and who was himself killed at twenty-four in the sky over Korea.

Leonard says that when members of the family declare they had come "West," they meant they had gone through the Cumberland Gap. At Oriole and Branchville they put down roots in their farms and graveyards, centers of life and history. Some gladly left laboring in rocky soil, boarding relatives who baked corn bread in sheets to feed their hounds, roguish neighbors, disease, and the death of children too frequent, when they heard footsteps in another sky—but they returned at last. Everything is doubly related. And for some, access to the life of the place has never grown over. "Come in, if you want to see how a poor man lives," said Mansfield's nephew when we knocked on his door. Mansfield had to laugh but shot back, "I know how a poor man lives."

25 : The Maze

All learning is entering the maze. Deeper and deeper you go, confiding in and made confident by your tutor at every step as you go on. You don't look back at first because you are engrossed and made to forget that there is such a thing as looking back. As you go on, your footsteps scroll up behind you, and you can never get them back—but you don't know that.

Mazes, knots, and gardens that are sets of enclosed rooms were invented in the Middle Ages, though the surviving ones are often much later constructions, undertaken in a restorative and self-conscious spirit, like the maze at Hampton Court, made in the late seventeenth century. By the eighteenth century it was considered amusing, though it retained trap possibilities. A watchman was set up on a high seat to oversee it and lead exhausted persons out. The early Hampton Court was itself a kind of maze, as poor Catherine Howard found when she eluded the guards at her chambers one night and ran down the darkened corridors, hair streaming, to find Henry and beg for her life. Too late, for Henry was already lost in the maze of Tudor power that had long separated him from the brightest Renaissance prince that ever came to the throne in England.

It's no accident that universities like Oxford and Cambridge look and feel like mazes, for their quadrangles originated in the cloisters of the monasteries from which organized learning began to separate in the ninth century. And cloisters were rooted in the enclosed Persian paradise garden, which still flourished in illuminations for such books as *The Romance of the Rose.* So even a little history here puts us in a maze, wondering whether these enclosed gardens are images of a delicate civilization putting battlements between itself and the barbarian forces outside or of contemplation serenely poised in the chaste pleasures of the mind or of an elegant and elaborate discourse on sexual love. Or all of these, one leading in some unforeseeable way into another.

And even when you begin to sense that you are in a maze, you can't help wanting to go on, to learn more. In his *Countrie Housewife's Garden* William Lawson provides you with patterns for knots and a maze. He knows you will want one. John Gerard says you can find the uncommon yellow arch-angel "under the hedge on the left hand as you go from the village of Hampsted neer London to the Church." This sounds easy to get to. In the same way, John Aubrey begins his notes on Hobbes by telling you that Hobbes was born "at his father's house in Westport, being that extreme house that points into or faces the horse-fair; the farthest house on the left hand as you go to Tedbury, leaving the church on your right." Hobbes is important, Aubrey implies; you will want to see where he was born. And you will—though it means learning to tell your right hand from your left.

Even poor Coyote, unredeemably foolish and impulsive, ordinarily un-able to learn, tried to undo his mistake and retrace his footsteps to go back and restore the wife he had lost, as Orpheus had, by his joyful, premature embrace. Back he went, the Nez Percé say, the way the tutoring death spirit had led him: going through the motions of admiring again the horses he couldn't see at the horse roundup place, of tasting imagined service berries, and of lifting the door flap of the still invisible "long, very very long lodge" to sit all day on the prairie in the sun and thirsty heat waiting for night and for the shadowy longhouse to separate itself from the darkness and brighten, with its many fires and the voices of ghost people whispering all around him—waiting to recognize his wife among those spirits. But of course the way back is not the same as the way to. Coyote only sat there in middle of the prairie. The story doesn't tell us what he learned—or what we learned, for that matter.

Yet we must tread the maze to learn. So the pilgrims, gathering in the church at Chartres, could walk their way through the maze inscribed on the floor of the nave as a foretaste of their pilgrimage. And both Mozart and Beethoven copied parts of the *Well-Tempered Clavier,* not (obviously) just to have a copy—Mozart could recall any piece of music after one hearing—but in order to relive or reembody in the acts of the hand Bach's original composition of the piece.

When I had to teach *Beowulf,* not having read it for some ten years, I had, at first, not to read secondary research on it or even study it but simply to read it every day for about seven days, until finally, when I went to bed, I dreamed it all night long. Then it was in my head—or I was in it. The linear order, the way in, had faded. Voices, gestures, and images were brightening, disengaging themselves from narrative, recognizing each other and linking in thoughtful ways: the mead hall, a bright island in the darkness, and the shadowy, recurring images in the background of the fight at Finnsburg and the fight at Ravenswood. Circles within circles appeared, for it takes the whole poem and the death of Beowulf finally to penetrate the center of the fight at Ravenswood, its cause, in a glimpse of the "old and terrible" king Ongentheow rescuing his wife, "old woman of times past." I had not begun to understand it, but I had taken a possible first step by acknowledging and embracing it as a maze.

The holy relic at Chartres was the tunic worn by the Virgin at the moment of the Annunciation, a token of such purity that no dead were ever buried in the church. Not even kings were allowed to see it, and when one demanded that the reliquary be opened, he was told that the keys could not be found. That he could ask such a thing demonstrated that he didn't have the key himself. Modern scholars puzzle over the deep well in the crypt and stories of a medieval *virgo paritura,* a wooden statue of a woman with a child in her lap. I for my part am amazed and confounded by the gifts in the treasury (among the gold, jewels, crowns, enameled roses innumerable) of a porcupine-skin belt bordered in silks, sent, they say, by the Huron tribe, and of the 11,000 porcelain beads representing the inhabitants of "new France," sent by the Abenaquis tribe. I can imagine the passage of silk and of porcelain beads from Europe to America, bought by rich furs, and even the women who worked these things into their own art. But I cannot follow the footsteps back to Europe through the minds of those who gave and those who received such gifts.

The gold-and-jewel-laden reliquary was opened during the Revolution, as you would expect, and its very ancient, Near Eastern silk veil exposed to rot and dispersal. One wonders why the church itself was not destroyed or defaced then as so many were. The answer is that it was saved by a modern maze, the committee, which deliberated long and probably confusedly about whether the building should become a shoe or soap manufactory, or some such thing—a decision not reached by the time the Revolution was over.

I certainly have not reached the high overview that the eighteenth century had of gothic churches. All the tutoring of books had not prepared me for my first sight of Chartres, which staggered me so that I couldn't even sense whether or not I was experiencing something great. And it has taken more than a week of years to begin to dream it. The vivid memory of this has made me sympathize with students bravely and innocently facing *Beowulf* or the *Iliad* for the first time. But I envy them a little, for they may find a rare archangel under a hedge as they go along.

Without aerial views or maps, the early inhabitants of Long Island knew that it was "Paumanok"—"fish-shaped." They walked over it until the island maze became a map. The thought of such power makes me feel like an outsider, though I live on this island. But if life is what can't leave anything behind, then we agree to the maze, and by going through with it, make sense of it at last. To thread the maze, I suppose, we must give up the way in. We embrace mazes in order to reembody what the tutoring spirits who once made them can teach us. Then the maze becomes the cathedral with its well water reaching to North America, becomes the *Iliad, The Well-Tempered Clavier.* The maze becomes a mantra.

26 : *Nadir*

Wintering at Walden, Thoreau's mind turned to images of sleep, to the past of the place and its losses, and to measuring. But since he condensed his two years at Walden into one when he wrote his book, he ended not with the end of a year's cycle, winter, but with the joyous chapters "Spring" and "Conclusion." I wonder what would have been the tone of the final chapters had he taken the point of view that another winter will eventually follow winter.

As a child I hated winter, as I hated all cold. It seemed to me I was always being thrust outdoors "to play," a bitterly incongruous idea to my mind. I thought that with more time indoors I could get a lot further in my reading. Then I might not have to read *The Count of Monte Cristo*, somewhat airlessly, under the bed covers by flashlight. It was clearly impossible to stop reading while the count was digging his way out of his dark dungeon.

It took being in the country to make me see how beautiful winter is. The lesser light of November, which I regretted every year, I began to perceive was somehow another light in which we could see other things. The slant of winter light lays a rose shine on gray bark and makes the dun bushes seem blond-matted, wheaty, or gold-lit. The fire of the sun lingers as a cool air-fire. The low sun stretches toward us in very long rays, and so distance becomes almost palpable. We can see far into the bare woods, almost to the former inhabitants.

I used to smile at William Cobbett on his "rural rides" through the southern counties of England making such frequent comparisons to the time of Richard II, as if Richard had been king in the age of Newton instead of in the age of Chaucer. As he rode to see the harvest in those years of 1822–26, Cobbett would reckon the region's former population from its manor houses, present and destroyed, and its churches, used or disused. But he was also always looking at the land itself and seeing in it a record of origins and of what men have done, as he does in this remarkable passage: "layers of stone at the bottom of hills of loam; the chalk first soft, then some miles farther on, becoming chalk-stone; then . . . burr-stone . . . and at last becoming hard, white stone, fit for any buildings, the sand-stone at Hindhead becoming harder and harder till it becomes nearly iron in Herefordshire, and quite iron in Wales; but indeed they once dug iron out of this very Hindhead."

He seems to start simply enough with observation of the land that lies before him. That land is the "piece of chalk" that Chesterton later found under his own feet. Then Cobbett's knowledge extends his observation out and away into Wales. But finally rushing into the same sentence, geology turns into human history as the present mining of Wales returns as the past time of "this very Hindhead." Is it chalk or iron then that lies under our feet? Solid stone or the story of human lives? It is both and all—the land is a space-time continuum, running beneath counties and countries and identifying them in the urgency of work.

Cobbett's energy pours into the crevices of November as he rises at five, rides all day in the rain and cold (he was in his sixties). At night, and after a meeting, he writes and posts off his report to London, "The Great Wen," sleeping then to rise at five the next morning. These rides and reckonings were part of his war with the government: its corn laws, money policy, and penal code. But aside from politics and persuasion, he always saw crops as part of the soil, as a man would who actually worked the soil. His descriptions make me wish I owned some of it myself: "the very best barley-land in the kingdom—a fine, buttery, stoneless loam, upon a bottom of sand or sand-stone." But it is more likely his powers of observation and metaphor I need.

At the other pole from Cobbett's love of experience are the intellectuals, who live more purely always in abstractions, in the country of no weather, their heads filled with physiology or geometry. Such men write books that in their greatness and silence correct societies too small yet for a new learning, societies with no honorable name for thinkers whose true mode is the subjunctive. The mathematician, Leonardo of Pisa, called "Fibonacci," was the son of "Bonaccio," a nickname meaning "good, stupid fellow," though this father was secretary of one of the new coastal factories and therefore an educated man in the twelfth century. Leonardo in his turn had been nicknamed "Bigollone," that is, "dunce, blockhead," which puts him in the class of another genius of the thirteenth century, Thomas Aquinas, dubbed "the speechless ox." Pisa at the end of the twelfth century, in many ways a cosmopolitan center, sounds in other ways rather like a provincial village.

At the beginning of the thirteenth century, the zenith of the Middle Ages, Leonardo published his first great work, *Liber abaci,* which contains traces of Greek, Arabian, and Indian mathematics and even, we're told, of Egyptian problems, revealing themselves "in the very numbers in which the problem is given, though," a commentator says, "one cannot guess through what channel they came to Leonardo's knowledge." It's fascinating to see Leonardo's chalk reaching back to Arab or Indian soil, and trace the iron he mined out of Egypt. And we *can* guess now. The channel must have been Arab Spain: tolerant, diverse, where Jews, Moslems, and Christians prospered together for centuries and were then making a high summer of learning and art.

When they are not put down as blockheads, the abstractors are often set aside as "absent-minded," perhaps because episodes of absence make good telling or because nothing is so memorable as the lack of mind in others. Aubrey says that William Harvey was with Charles I at Edgehill. During the fight, "the Prince and Duke of Yorke were committed to his care. He told me that he withdrew with them under a hedge, and tooke out of his pockett a booke and read; but he had not read very long before a Bullet of a great Gun grazed on the ground neare him, which made him remove his station." The discoverer of the circulation of the blood is not a practical man, we sense. He seems uninterested in the blood of the heirs to the throne—or in his own, for that matter. Yet Harvey was more "minded," surely, than those who were firing the bullets. We remember that the "most excellent genius" of William Lawes was quenched at the battle of Chester in 1645—and he, at age forty-three, with still-unexpressed music in his head.

Aubrey is no dummy, however. He admires Harvey's lack of worldliness and records it as a sign of his aptness for thought: "He did delight to be in the dark, and told me he could then best contemplate. He had a house . . . in Surrey, a good aire and prospect, where he had Caves made in the earth, in which in Summer time he delighted to meditate." An amazing idea, that a man in summer with "aire and prospect" preferred dark caves and went to the expense of creating them. But then, seventeenth-century England changed our ideas of dark and light in more than one way.

It's no surprise that the melancholy Dowland counted himself part of the circle of Lucy, Countess of Bedford, whose dark beauty and serious mind seemed to suit the feast day of her patron saint on December thirteenth, which in the old calendar was the winter solstice, the longest night of the year. "Semper Dowland, Semper Dolens" was Dowland's own title for a retrospective lute piece. "Down, down," sings the tenor in another one of his songs, "leaning into" the note, skewing and wrenching it in a foretelling of the ending where the repeat, "Down and arise, down and arise," becomes "down and arise I never shall." Donne's "Nocturnal" for Lucy plunges to the nadir with all the abstractions at his command, plenty of verbs in the subjunctive, and strong pauses after words like "shadow":

> If I an ordinary nothing were,
> As shadow, a light and body must be here.
>
> But I am none, nor will my sun renew.

And from the "down" point in the poem, indeed Donne does not "arise." Having linked *sun* with *none* in an internal rhyme, he leaps out of the natural cycle altogether, leaving it, as if it were worth very little, to "you lovers."

For us in New York the winter has plenty of sunlight—no constant cloud cover to warm us, or gloom us either. The sun freezes us. At the latitude of Madrid, we are not so far north as England. In January the sun draws me out from under my covers—where I might be meditating—to an irresistible walk on the dam at the reservoir. The day is at zero; the sunshine dazzling everywhere. The wind is almost a gale, boisterous, in its highest spirits, blowing yesterday's snow almost down into my lungs. I don't know why I lean into it and go on, except that the water of the reservoir is deep blue and leaping into whitecaps. It's deep enough now to cover the tree stumps and stone walls of the villages it flooded when the idea of circulating mountain water through New York City overwhelmed the idea of a self-contained village. I could throw a piece of chalk now from my schoolteacher's pocket into the water that will flow into the drinking glass of the concert master of the orchestra rehearsing this week at Lincoln Center. At the prospect of a walk into this wind I am daunted and freezing. Yet I can't turn my back on all that natural energy, and Leonard tells me afterwards that I have seriously damaged my claims to hate winter.

Thanks to our North American light, I don't have to accept Donne's dichotomy of the natural and the spiritual, and I have plenty of my own experience of the subjunctive. I have started a thrilling book of analysis, from among the hundreds offered every year in this wide world, and I want to throw out my clock and stay up late reading it through the long night—though I might regret it if tomorrow turns out to be the morning when Haydn, an ordinary man and a hard-working musician, plans to make the very first sun rise in a full orchestral C major.

27 : *Cat's Cradle*

In the winter the garden gets to be a garden of the mind, though perhaps it was always that. It emerges as metaphor, the kind of thing the mind can't live without—metaphor, I mean. Here in the north there is no winter gardening. A place near us, beautifully landscaped with broad-leaf and needle evergreens, looks the same in winter as in summer. This is very well in winter, but has perhaps a faint memorial quality in seasons of growth.

My garden, meanwhile, looks barren. Without snow and bared to the cold, its stalk and leaf litter reveal to the guilty gardener what she failed to care for when it was flourishing. I imagine it as wholly potential now, just an underground system: tap roots, their tender tips hardened, the mass of rootlets shrunken, and the stems that behave like roots—the bulbs, tubers, rhizomes, and corms that foster their buds underground. They seem both tough and tenuous.

I trust in their vigor because I can't do anything else. I recall Wordsworth's "Heavy as frost, and deep almost as life," with its poignant pause or poise on the word "almost," and think of the margin life occupies, surviving just below the frost. Of course the root is not marginal, but a tough, well-engineered system of life, as Asa Gray describes it, with powers of "assimilation, growth, storage, distribution of its centers, and seasonal reformation," hidden from us but the source of all the life we see.

Wordsworth seemed able to recall the roots of his life in its sensations in an astonishing way. His metaphor is not earthy: root and plant, but watery: source and river or ocean and shore. That was appropriate for a man who could return, in sensation or vision, to his source and see it again, in contrast to most of us whose lives are rooted in the dark. But Leonard's father said he could remember what he had done on each of his birthdays as a child. On his sixth birthday he had helped his cousin clear the brush and weeds out of a fence row. On his seventh birthday he had walked down the road to visit his aunt.

The fact of his remembering such things is as remarkable as the things are commonplace. Children of my day would only have recalled something special: a trip to Louisville, a party of friends, a longed-for gift. But there seem not to have been parties and gifts, and the child made the birthday himself by notching in his mind the contentment of an ordinary day as an unforgettable happiness.

The happiness I remember as a child is being alive and leisurely in my own purposes: blue October, minding the burning leaves in the gutter, or summer afternoons, walking alone down the sidewalk listening to the mourning doves, before I had a word like "poignant." Places and things met my sense of them as an answering reality. One day was life, if I had the patience of the fire smouldering in the leaves, the light on the porcelain tub, the delicate stiffness of ironed cotton, the flecks on a cold apple, water standing in a glass in its own watery light. Life was the time when nothing happened, only life taking place.

Most children must experience this, and perhaps it accounts for the way even extremely deprived children, living amidst events that paralyze adults, give a little skip on their way down the street and are happy. How this changes I suppose we can't remember, but slowly, as there get to be too many events for sense to carry. Life begins to be narrative and history. Yet we hope that we don't simply leave childhood but become adults, that we do not lose sensation but develop mind. If all goes well with us, we don't have to divide ourselves from experience. Though we experience what's been called "the separation of the knower from the known," in this separation we find we can examine what we know.

This kind of consciousness takes a long time in history to develop. Our preliterate ancestors found it advantageous to free up some brain space by bestowing in writing some of their crucial societal knowledge, like patrilineal lines and who sent what ships to Troy. The Greeks began with the alphabet, and so do we. They could do this because some stonecutters and potters invented the Greek alphabet, the only true alphabet, and so revolutionized the power of persons in the West to advance in science and democracy. The effect was transforming, but as you would expect, there's something special about the development of the invention itself. The invention of the alphabet was a conceptual act, "an act of intellect." Scholars said this when they realized that the Greeks conceived the idea of consonants, a kind of underground component of utterable language.

Other writing systems were syllabaries, that is, symbols for sets of sounds. Within these sets there was as yet no such thing as "vowel" or "consonant." Each set was merely one pronounceable sound. Some scripts (like the North Semitic) are unvocalized and show similar ways of starting and stopping a sound. Others (like the Mycenean Linear B) are vocalized; they include the sound along with its starting or stopping. In all such syllabaries there could be hundreds of symbols. Learning and using them would take so much of an adult's time that writing would belong only to an elite class of specialists, and the kind of thinking that writing promotes would be learned only by the privileged.

The Greeks did not make the alphabet by inventing vowels for the Phoenician syllabary, as people used to say. They took a real leap of mind in order to conceive something beyond sense experience. They invented the idea of consonants, things that can't be heard. As Plato says, consonants are "mute": *aphona, aphthonga.* So the "consonant" is first of all a concept, an act of abstraction springing beyond what sense can tell us. This silent but conceivable thing helps to give speech to the thing that is almost unspeakable because it is so deeply conceived.

A real alphabet changes a culture profoundly and politically by making universal literacy a possibility. Eric Havelock defines the brilliance of the invention: "The Greek symbols had succeeded in isolating with economy and precision the elements of linguistic sound and had arranged them in a short atomic table learnable in childhood." Twenty-six characters, learnable in childhood, the fibrous roots for absorbing and distributing knowledge.

What you have can be stored. And what you have socially—how to call an assembly or hold funeral games—can be stored orally, in the memory of oral tradition. But how do you save what you have lost? Oral cultures cannot afford to do this. To save what you have lost is extremely difficult without writing, especially for the individual. The problem is not remembering loss (God knows), but expressing it. Coming to terms with it, as we say.

We want to make sense of loss within our whole life. To do this, we try to give it a body, not fleshly, but still material, a body of sense. We speak, write, paint, play music, project the loss somehow into work and experience, because it's experience that feels like life. We give loss a body to make it whole within our lives, make our lives whole with it. To reseal our lives without the loss and so discard it would be to lessen our lives and corrupt our imagination. And the imagination's work is precisely to raise loss up incorruptible.

Two of my friends, and my mother, lost sons. One friend lost two sons, ten years apart. The mother's loss of a child is unbearable—her identity as a mother was to bear him in the first place. When one of these women, a musician, told me she had written a series of poems as she tried to work out her grief, I asked to read them. She gave them to me readily, and I saw that they were not private effusions but real poems. Like speech, they were public, but they had been worked into speech by a person writing.

I think often of Greek and Roman steles I've seen. I found it hard to learn to see them, they are so quiet. None of the rage and drama of loss is there. The quietness seems to grow deeper in the pause of the moment of farewell they all memorialize. They express an imagined moment, for seldom does the departing wife, taking her infant with her, touch her husband's hand so. Nor does the strong standing young man, his head inclined in resignation under the curving top of the stone, just touch the fingers of his parents in joining and release. Animals lose and grieve, apparently. We others separate ourselves from grief in order to live, but we conceive the loss in order to bear it.

"The peculiarity of living things," says Asa Gray, "is their power of transforming matter into new forms." I think about this as I consider the dictionary picture of an Inuit woman with a cat's cradle on her fingers. Cat's cradle must have been the offspring of woman's and man's work of netting, knotting, knitting, a game invented to teach children those hand skills, keeping their wits sharp in the pleasure of a game. In it, we are told, "the string is transferred from the fingers of one to those of another, at each transfer with a change of form."

28 : *Elation*

The crunch of winter when work intensifies, twelve-hour days and work weekends are commonplace, everything goaded on by deadlines. Then the temptation to idleness, even an hour of it, sets in seriously. I want to spend an hour at a bare table, looking at a small sake cup, the man and woman depicted at the bottom of it clearly frivolous in their gold-dotted robes, or at old prints of courtesans dressed as samurai, whatever play with the heroic that denotes.

A high treat would be a prowl through an old bookstore with my friend Marie. We're cheerful simply at our prospects as we look about. We don't need to buy anything; yet the world lies all before us. We're thrilled at the sales, for though we're not poor students anymore, our thrift goes deep. Signs on the tables say, "All novels: $1.00!" We look them over to approve the store owner's enterprise, but perfunctorily, because novels don't charm us. We head for the poetry and the nonfiction shelves, and I quicken my pace. Beyond are the dictionaries, and here I catch my breath as I sense my blood hastening into its arteries. I stand among them anticipating the matchless interest of their expert and elegant definitions. Vast abstract concepts, impossible to grasp almost, will be concisely seized and expressed, not one feather of their gorgeous plumage ruffled. "Catenary," for example, is:

The shape assumed
by a perfectly flexible
inextensible
infinitely fine cord
in equilibrium under given forces.
It is the locus
of the focus
of a parabola rolling on a straight line.

To the question, "What book would you take on a deserted island?" one of my friends would answer, "Shakespeare." But I have long known I would take *Webster's Second* and *Third International.* Then, having time at last, I could glimpse the worlds of learning epitomized there—not systematically, but threading my way along through language as one word leads to another. I would discover that, as I suspected all along, everything is finally connected. Reading Locke's dictum, "Nothing in the intellect that was not previously in sense perception," I could linger in the bliss of Leibnitz's reply, *"nihil nisi intellectus ipse,"* "nothing that is not in the intellect itself," intimating, as the dictionary author says, "that some knowledge is derived by the intellect from its own structure." I would be fearless with Kantianism ("which see") and Aristotelianism and entelechy ("which see") knowing that once well started, there would be no need ever to stop.

But if my friend had all of Shakespeare, it would be only fair for me to have Johnson's *Dictionary* too in my deserted-island backpack. Johnson's *Dictionary* is often made game of, but in fact it is the supreme dictionary because the depth of its definitions is refined out of a learning both massive and intelligent and balanced in the most delicate discrimination. Even an excellent dictionary feels a little thin after it.

There are seventeen definitions for "fair," for example. Johnson distinguishes between "mild; not compulsory" ("being by fair means wrought thereunto") and "mild; not severe" ("remit / To life obscur'd, which were a fair dismission"). We recognize "equitable; not injurious" ("His doom is fair, / That dust I am, and shall to dust return"). And of course "beautiful; elegant of feature," used of a woman's face. But beyond the simple charm of definition, there's something more satisfying here. The plenitude of meanings and the clarity of their discernment express what it is like to think, if we could only sustain it long enough to get good at it.

Johnson can define what most people would only gesture at: to knit is "to make or unite by texture without a loom." So you can see the real power of dictionaries is that they stand against the trivial but insidious objection that some words—and some concepts—don't have to be defined at all, because their meaning is self-evident. Socrates never brings Meno to the realization that Meno cannot define "virtue" though he admits he can't define what we might call a lesser concept, "shape." When Socrates defines "shape" ("the only thing that always accompanies color"), Meno labels the definition "naive," a barely veiled evaluation of Socrates' whole stance, which had begun with an admission of ignorance. It wouldn't tax Johnson's powers of irony to define "naive" in this context.

Above all on my deserted island I'd have time to wander through the etymologies of the dictionary, leading to the metaphors at the roots of all words. For if words lead to philosophy on one side, they lead to poetry on the other. There is "salt" (*salus*) in "salary," originally the allowance given Roman soldiers to buy salt. And there is "bread" in "company," companions being those with whom you share bread (*panis*). The understructure of witty poems is the ironic play of the metaphors latent in the roots of the words. The best example is the work of Emily Dickinson.

I think of her bat, the "elate philosopher," whenever we glimpse the bats on a summer evening. Elate—"lifted up"—they are, swooping in an "arc . . . inscrutable," the very parabola of the natural philosopher. One night at dinner Leonard mentioned that he'd seen a bat floating in the rain barrel. He thought it was alive, he said, but it turned out that he had not abstracted it, so I grabbed the slotted spoon and went on the run. Sure enough, there it was, but so small I'd have thought it an old leaf. I scooped it out, alive still, and hung it up on the porch to dry. Not quite sodden, it had spread out its wings to keep afloat in an unfamiliar element. And the wings had served. It had kept its elation, the clever thing, by trusting in its eccentric genius: the only mammal with true flight. The summer air restored it, I'm sure, to its evening companions skimming the insects over the old pear tree after the veery has quit, and the bat brightens the dusk with its quick energy, though "not a song pervade its lips / —Or none perceptible." Quite a shrewd guess of Dickinson's at the sound we now know bats emit, their latent song or sonar, imperceptible to our earth-bound ears.

Late last October, when I went to deliver a message to my new neighbor, Mark, I found him mucking about at the bottom of his dried-up pond. For a moment I was concerned that he might excavate some frogs, remit to life obscur'd as they are in the winter earth. The end of the season of gardening had left him idling a bit, scrutinizing the pond sediment while he waited for his fair wife to drive up from the city.

We sat in his unheated house, the door wide open to the cool October air and the sight of the pond. He began to tell me about the soil in the pond bottom, what he'd learned about it, rubbing thumb and fingers together to illustrate its peculiar graininess. I of course was as fascinated as he and found myself listening more intently, with mounting interest, imagining the possibilities from the color of the dirt on his fingers and the muck dotting his boots. My weekend work left for half an hour on my desk, my oatmeal bread rising under its white towel faded altogether from my consciousness. Then it struck me as hilarious. What would an onlooker think?—two people sitting there talking ardently about dirt, knowing they'd struck an inexhaustible subject.

Well, we can't know what will elate us, what stir us and lead us on to thought and work. The dust of the earth itself may be the thing, fundamental as bread and salt, filled in its own way with the sediments of history as words are. There can be, probably, no more intrinsic interest in the one than in the other—if knowledge is at least partly derived by the intellect from its own structure. When Hektor is giving Paris one of his scolds, Paris accepts the part that is fair, but rejects the other, saying, "Yet do not / bring up against me the sweet favors of golden Aphrodite." There is wisdom and grace in all things, it seems:

> Never to be cast away are the gifts of the gods, magnificent,
> which they give of their own will, no man could have them
>   for wanting them.

Everyone knows the experience of looking up and encountering the gaze of a stranger—it may be from way down the aisle on a bus, too far away for the gaze to have been "audible." I love faces and I like public transportation for the chances it gives me to study the range of the human countenance. But, knowing that a person's gaze penetrates another person's concentration even on a good book, I'm prepared for the instant of return awareness, which I sense and look aside from just before the owner of the face looks up to find me, a glance I can see clearly out of the corner of my eye.

You'd think that science, which can hurl its thought into outer space and back to the beginning of our time, could investigate such a well-known phenomenon. But it hasn't formulated any concepts for the power of sending sight toward another person—the *coup d'oeil*—nor for the mysterious consciousness of an "eye touch." And even more mysterious, for the mirror-infinity of the awareness of an awareness.

Perhaps the fault is in psychology, for what we need is not behaviorists or students of repression but astrophysicists of the mind who can conceive of a psyche as a cosmos of forces like electromagnetism. Perhaps the gaze is a kind of "strong" force, though Leonard Deen, my expert on the cosmos, says the force is gravitation, the pull of the "orbs" of the eyes.

Painters since the Renaissance have done better than scientists. There's a small Rembrandt in Boston, a self-portrait, "The Artist In His Studio," out of which the painter, in the act of painting, looks at you with his usual, disconcerting gaze. After a moment you realize that Rembrandt is in fact looking at himself in a mirror that you can't see. Were you in the room with him, with no change of stance, you'd be seeing the unportrayed him and the blind back of the canvas, upon the front of which he is inscribing an identity only he can see while he is conceiving it.

The sensory power of the painting, however, makes you step back out of the canvas and restores the first appearance. He *is* looking at you. But now you know more, because there's no way of arresting this stepping in and out of the canvas. The painter has let you watch him look at you with the same look he gives to himself in his most alone moments. You know more, though it's not science, but an intuition that art has made richer—both more surprising and more certain, an intuition that loves intelligence.

Last summer I met the friend of a friend with his young family, a child psychiatrist and therapist, who appeared to be a thoughtful, pleasantly straightforward person. The accidents of restaurant seating placed us next to each other, and after we'd scanned the menu, I determined to ask him an important question before our acquaintance went any further—while his answer could be taken as a disinterested contribution to knowledge. "The question is, " I said, "do you believe in love at first sight?" To do him credit, he took this very well—caught only for a moment over a possible protest at the question's unscientific nature or at its having been kidnapped by romancers. I looked at his beautiful, intelligent wife and the beautiful children, while he considered, I suppose, the hopelessly ambiguous stance of any answer. Then he just took it seriously and simply as I had asked it and said, "Yes, I guess I do."

It was love at first sight for Benjamin Haydon when he saw the Elgin marbles in his student days. In 1808 the marbles were still in limbo, stored in a "damp, dirty pent-house . . . ranged within sight and reach." No one could be prepared for the first sight of them, and Haydon was astonished. "The first thing I fixed my eyes on was the wrist of a figure . . . in which were visible . . . the radius and ulna. [Then] I darted my eye to the elbow, and saw the outer condyle visibly affecting the shape." In another figure he saw "the muscle shown under the one arm-pit in that instantaneous action of darting out." He was seeing for the first time the original fusion of an ideal beauty and the natural. He got permission to study them and drew "ten, fourteen, and fifteen hours at a time; staying often till twelve at night, holding a candle and my board in one hand and drawing with the other."

Without any such informing knowledge of anatomy, I saw the marbles in their grand room in the British Museum, so easy of access that if you had enough sense to be staying in Bloomsbury, you could dash in every day and visit them first thing before any of your other expeditions. The friezes of the cavalry held me: the endlessly moving horses and riders bestriding them, some figures so energetic they seemed to emerge from the marble at one moment and then move effortlessly out of it, lifting with an urgency that has no hurry in it but simply expresses their youthful power, at one with their animals and suspended there—the idea of motion visible.

You see it is partly the wearing away of the marble that creates this effect; its minute execution seems to be gone. But in fact the details have so informed the depth that you can see them anyway. And the "depth" is imagined, for the sculptures are reliefs, about two inches deep. The idea of the sculpture was never in its finish, anyway, but in what the Greeks call *telos*, or purpose, the end that is there in the beginning.

It was a similar kind of ideal beauty that struck my neighbor Mark in an "organic" bakery one day. Not seeing anyone in the store, he said, he ventured into the kitchen where he was met with the vision of three beautiful young women kneading bread. This was classical if not archetypal. "But what did you think?" I said. "I thought," he replied, "'I *must* get a job here.'" Since one of these young women became his wife, he was a good candidate for my question about love at first sight. As it happened this vision was fateful for him in more than one way, for food and especially baking became his profession.

My research, happily, is quite unprofessional, though it is almost lifelong. I am at leisure with my data and feel no urgency to interpret them. It is of course continually instructive, part of the question of how we know what we know as the intuitive certainties we trust our lives to and how those chains of information, association, selection, and reasoning are condensed at lightning speed, at a glance—through a mere current of air, it seems— and issue as what we see, from the end of the affair, to have been correct.

My love of faces is a part of my pleasure in teaching—character inscribed on faces, never the same, ranging from those animated by speech or vivid attention to those sinking gently into sleep. The countenances may be read but not interpreted. Like Haydon I have long days when I work at them ten or twelve hours and come home, like him, to a soothing cup of tea to think about the glories I have seen—though, fortunately, with more than one candlepower of illumination.

One face, that of a former student, caught my attention the other day as I was going down and he was going up the stairs. I stopped to ask him how he did, and we lingered there, talking catercorner at each other about his writing classes, his writing, and the antinomy between them. He had just discovered García Lorca's *The Poet in New York* and recommended it to me.

As we spoke, classes let out, and students began going down between us. We continued our conversation, clustering our sentences to dart bundles out when gaps appeared. The exchange superseded the interference. We didn't move to the same side, poised as we were comfortably face to face. Students started to come up from below now, and more students came down. We raised our voices somewhat to hurl our word bundles at each other.

Finally Leonard himself came down, trailed by a student still talking to him. We looked at each other, amused by our reflective stances. He went on down, and Justin and I signed off after a moment or two more, he promising to leave me the name of another good book he'd just found. I went down with the flow of students and found Leonard waiting below. We walked together back to our offices across the campus, and he paused to point out to me New York in the distance, standing out like an old photograph, under a gray sky but in air very clear.

Year Five

30 : *High Summer*

Driving out of the heat wave, north into a clearing blue, into a stiffening wind from the northwest: high sky, high clouds, and all the green below in the tossing trees getting more intense for the clarity of the blue. When we reach the fields tilting back to the uprising of Mohonk, the cloud shadows roam across them as darker green. In the windy sunlight the fields and trees sparkle deep in a color we have no name for. The sky blue seems to strike a chord with the blue in the leaves to bring out the gold remainder, the gold that Frost says the green was in the beginning.

The ides of July—it's high summer, but gone at its height. Mornings at nine the sun just barely touches the fenced-in garden. And the day is just lightening at five in the morning. Yet we anticipate summer as the supreme present. Long days of high light we imagine, when all our plans will be in act, in the energy of presence. This summer I thought I'd learn a little Spanish, just memorize a few poems to get a sense of words, word order, and idiom. I'd also poke around in the Middle Ages a bit. Those enterprises, my regular work, and a garden project would fill up summer days nicely.

And after our work day there'll still be a long twilight. It would be like sitting on a terrace after dinner in June in some country like Portugal at the western end of its time zone. The sun would be setting behind our backs, shining on something we are looking at—say a little hill with three or four white-walled, tile-roofed houses set into it. About ten-thirty, in the after-glow, they begin to look like a Pissarro. The walls take the sun's gold, and the tile roofs become the red of some other language, where red lasts longer: *les toits rouges*—glowing not just with the luminosity of the sun but with the human perception of paint on canvas.

We seem to have two sunrises here in the country, which in their way foster the sense of a long day. In the first, the sun crests the tip of the far ridge, beaming between the trunks of our ridge trees, and levels through the bedroom window to lay a rose light on the white wall. Later the sun rises over our own trees and shines on the eastern edge of the small meadow. How long the interval is we realized on the night of the two moon risings. We left the city in a storm clearing and watched a large orange moon, one day past the full, rise rapidly over Throgs Neck. She had just got above our ridge trees two and a half hours later when we arrived in Atwood. We had the odd sense that we'd taken a flight west, across the ocean, racing the earth spin, to arrive at the hour of our departure.

In a way summer is the time of annuals. The perennials make their various sorts of growth in spring and fall, and what you get in summer from them is a kind of inheritance. But the principle of annuals is continuous growth. They want no check in their headlong, annular course: to end as a seed, where they began. The lettuce holds off from the natural bitterness of its chicory self only so long as it has steady water and enough ammonia to make the protein it keeps moving onward to growing parts. Beans mustn't be stopped a minute. Even some bare stalks, their seedling leaves eaten this spring by a predator, are flowering anyway to get to their goal of *beans*.

Tomatoes and zucchini are tropical and love heat, spreading leaves eighteen or sixteen inches long (and twenty-one inches wide for the zucchini), setting, elongating, or rounding their fruit with a skin suppler than silk, tight against outside forces and expanding with their inner water of growth. They chuckle during hot nights, waiting for me to get out there in the morning and give them more water, their due, and in due amounts. When my bedroom can't cool off before four in the morning, I would sleep better outside among the plants and their humming plans for the next day's cambrium advance, lulled by the flow in xylem and phloem, and given good dreams by the dark that has quieted their breathings.

Such a small thing separates us, one thing out of four: nitrogen. I cannot make amino acids, the proteins that nevertheless form, as Asa Gray says, my "flesh and sinews and the animal parts of the bones." Though I am organic, I cannot, in fact, originate any organic matter. Moreover, no part of my fabric is starch or sugar, though my body uses them to live. But the fabric of plants is carbon, hydrogen, and oxygen, in the proportion $(C_6H_{12}O_6)_n$: starch. Gray says that "starch is to cellulose or vegetable fabric just what the prepared clay is to the potter's vessel—the same thing, only requiring to be shaped and consolidated." Nitrogen is no part of their tissue, though they can assimilate it from ammonia and, along with carbonic acid and water, form proteins for growing cells.

All animal life depends on plants. It's almost a social duty to water them, especially since water is not just drink to them, does more than fill their tissue. Hydrogen and oxygen are two of the inorganic materials they transform into organic life. So this summer when sixty days of rain hung over the Mississippi, and sixty days and more of no rain and blazing sunshine has been our lot in Atwood, I use my two sunrises to coax water out of my slow-running well for the annuals going full blast and for the perennials of my new garden projects. I watch the water running through the grains of my sandy soil, to which years of mulching and composting have only added enough organic matter to keep the grains apart for a season before it decays altogether. I wonder whether it's possible to add clay to sand without getting cement.

The growth of annuals suggests that summer is not so much long as intense. We are not vegetative. Long summer days are too few for us to get the hang of or bear in mind. The summer goes, and my Spanish is pretty quiet. But I comfort myself with my humanness, for if the future is in all my present moments by anticipation, so is the past in my present—and more of it than I have lived, thank goodness—rising like a spring out of a water table laid down in the Pleistocene age. I hear it in words and in music where a very old strain or invention persists like an inexhaustible inheritance. The pseudo-Italian name of the passacaglia cannot veil its origin in *passacalla,* a guitar tune played passing through the streets. It has passed through countries and centuries by now in the shape given it by an early sixteenth-century Spanish harpist: a rhythmic patterning over a descending bass, a four-note theme.

And this Ludovico, who had only a diatonic harp with one row of strings, was one of those whose improvising style gave rise to the toccata (*toccare,* "to touch") with its rapid finger work and what have been called "daring harmonic clashes." One wonders how he achieved these without a row of chromatic strings, but he did it by inventing technique to transcend the material limits of his instrument: stopping the strings with one hand to make a passing sharp, one writer says, and probably with "cunning *scordatura,*" unusual tuning. Perhaps I can learn to tune my well, though cunning indeed would be the *scordatura* that could overcome its stubborn flow of one half gallon a minute and a half hour of watering before the pump loses its prime.

In the meantime a short easy poem asks me:

> ¿Dices que nada se crea?
> No te importe, con el barro
> de la tierra, haz una copa
> para que beba tu hermano.

Well, I'm not worried about creating anything new, not this summer anyway. And where, Machado, will I get the clay to make the cup to give my brother—and my sister too—a drink? But he is a persistent person, this poet.

> ¿Dices que nada se crea?
> Alfarero, a tus cacharros.
> Haz tu copa y no te importe
> si no puedes hacer barro.

I am to make my cup and it doesn't matter if I cannot make the clay. And there is something spirited about his call, "Alfarero, a tus cacharros": Potter, to your machine!—your wheel or your well. If I water my vegetables, doubtless they will make my clay for me. I have been watering the lettuce, perhaps foolishly because it's past its prime. But I rather like its bitterness, the presence of its original spirit, not quite tamed by two centuries of improved futures.

31 : *Experts*

I once met a gardening expert at a party of journalists and public affairs experts. She was a beautiful young woman, newly married, newly come to this country, wonderfully confident, and already writing a gardening column for her local newspaper. Her conversation, I noticed, was mostly about her column, natural enough in that group.

When she turned to her garden, she told me about fungicides and the problems she was having with her roses—black spot and all. Nothing seemed to work; she was trying stuff with the soil, burning every leaf that fell, and so on. I suddenly got a picture of her roses and without thinking said, "Are you growing them in a house corner, facing south?" "Why, yes," she said. "How did you know? What does that mean?" "Well," I said, "roses really like lots of air all around, don't they? Otherwise they get those funguses. We imagine them as southern, needing protection here. But they like a little mound out in the middle of the yard with breezes."

I have no expertise in roses—hardly any interest in them, in fact—but an image had come to me of a round bed of roses in a park near the house I lived in as a girl. The bed was indeed out in the middle of an open space and on the highest ground. The roses were always tossing in a breeze, flourishing without spot or taint, though I never saw anybody tending them. I used to wonder how they survived the cold Michigan winters unsheltered out there. But in their own paradise they appeared naturally sound, proof against the evils of the weather.

At the party, as we spoke, I discovered that the young woman had, in fact, never gardened before. She wanted to do some journalism, and the local paper had needed a garden column. She had obviously known that was not beyond the powers of a woman of intelligence and common sense and jumped right in. She was a born expert, really, and went on I'm sure to wider fields, to the benefit of the public.

I consulted a garden expert one time when I lived in my first own house. This friend is a man of choice language, reserved, ironic, and thoroughly kind. I knew gardeners were supposed to have compost piles, and so I had one. But I didn't exactly know what you were supposed to do with one—not in the middle of the growing season anyway—so I made up my mind to ask John. My question flabbergasted him. He was speechless. Too many things came to his lips at once, some of them exclamations unutterable, I suppose. The idea that someone could have a compost pile, that gardener's chief desire, a rich gold mine, and then apparently not know how to use it struck him dumb.

I myself became an expert once by accident when a colleague, newly housed and gardened, asked me what vine he should plant in a certain spot. I was sorry to say I knew nothing about vines, though naturally I had read about them at one time or another. He didn't seem to hear my disclaimer. He had it firmly in his mind that this was my métier. He himself was an expert in his field, and he wanted one in gardening. I mumbled something about Taylor, all the time thinking that he was not about to do research in vines, and it was probably up to me to do it—though I didn't have time for the task either. I think we left the question up in the air.

About a year and a half later I ran into him, and he thanked me heartily for the good advice I had given. The vine—whatever it was—had turned out perfectly, he said. I scarcely knew what to say. A protest formed on my lips, but I quelled it. We were in some realm of fiction, evidently, and I would have to accept credit I didn't deserve. So I smiled and said I was very glad he had got what he wanted.

Waiting for the palaces of Alhambra to open one night about nine-thirty, I met a born expert in peoples of the South and of the North, a young engineer from Tenerife. A sober, reserved person, he had been very kind about steering us to the right place for tickets. Then in the quiet, watching the sun go down, he said, as if on a confessional impulse, "The Spanish are the best people, after all—so open, sociable, people of the South. We are out of doors so much, talking with each other, emotional, enjoying our-selves." Not at all like those Germans and English, it turns out, up there in the North, in the dark and rainy cold, huddled inside their houses, apart and solitary.

I laughed and said only, "But surely, if one wants to study, to learn, to get ahead in the world, one has to stay inside a good deal and read?" I felt like asking him whether he had ever been to London, where the populace is more gregarious even than Sevillians, as far as I can see, spilling out of pubs without benefit of café tables or warm weather, over the sidewalks into the streets, beer in one hand while they gesticulate with the other as an aid to constant talk, in a manner markedly southern, you might say. I simply passed over the extent of emotional and passionate British literature.

But I wanted to ask him whether he had seen the gardens of England, for however beautiful the gardens of Alhambra—and they are certainly a version of Paradise in their formal perfection, their endless series of rose gardens, the deep gorge they border, and above all in the way they run with water—the gardens of Britain are incomparable in their freedom, their inexhaustible variety of species, and in their imaginative power. One mustn't compare, however, I reminded myself the next day as I set my ear to the wall of the summer palace and heard it thrum with water.

You glimpse Paradise now and then, gratefully, at unexpected moments: the first surprised gaze into Canyon de Chelly or the alluvial fields Leonard spotted down off a road in Portugal. On one side of the road a spring ran out of the steep rock into a cistern where folks could catch it. On the other side, forty feet down, ran a stream amidst the rich land it had laid down: a "narrow room." Long plots lay along it, deep in green, too small to be called fields, too serious to be called gardens.

A woman was cultivating and thinning—what? Corn or sorghum, I couldn't tell. She worked rapidly, creating the order of the place as she went, not rows, but an all-over pattern. Her feet were bare, and noticing that made me see the richness of the black soil. She was saving her shoes, obviously, but I could feel the pleasure of having one's feet in such earth. At one point she looked up at us from her work. I scarcely knew how to acknowledge her regard, or my own, except to raise my hand in a kind of salute. Later I took some pictures, for the light was favorable.

This reminded me of the times I used to teach two weeks of *Paradise Lost* in an all-purpose, introductory poetry course. How interested some of my colleagues were then in the figure of Satan. One of them assured me that students understood Milton best through the idea of rebellion, and I had no reason to doubt her. She and her students went into Satan pretty thoroughly, she said. I was interested in Paradise, as you might imagine, seen in its human genesis and in the prophetic energy of joy and woe, for I suppose Milton does not see Paradise as history but as a once-home, nor in retrospect but in a surge of mythic presence and power.

At any rate, in those two weeks I used to walk into class and find a few ringers sitting casually in the back row, in their baseball jackets. Once one of them strolled in from the hall in the middle of class. He happened to be passing, I suppose, and heard some of the poetry. I didn't lecture—they were perfectly simple-minded sessions working close to the language of the poem.

When Eve took the fruit of the knowledge of good and evil—"Forth reaching to the fruit, she plucked, she eat . . . / And knew not eating death," and when Adam, meeting her, sees the roses he has gathered for her wither in her presence, the ringers departed. Before Adam and Eve left the incomparable air of Paradise. It was interesting, I thought, that the young men wanted to study for a few days in their youth, Paradise in the light of its loss. Too hard to keep, I thought, when none of my pictures of the stream gardens came out. Camera, film, and the developing process had been unequal to the riverine fields of a small stream in Portugal on a morning early in June.

The first fruits of the garden have come in, and you can see why certain cultures have thought it right to sacrifice them, set them apart in some way. There is something sacred about their perfection. I can see the down on the beans as I pick them. It's enough—luxury enough—to serve them just picked and barely cooked, ranged on a platter, dribbled delicately with good olive oil. The cucumbers have a startling sweetness to them. Zucchini the size of clubs are silken. Tomatoes come in warm from the sun, and we realize, as we do every year, that their taste cannot be imagined or remembered.

I hate to see the plants exchange the vigorous green of their leaves for ripe fruit—even for tomatoes—though I seem unable to prevent it. One week the plants are fountains of beautiful pungent leaves, green globes burgeoning among them. The next week when the first tomatoes turn red, the lower leaves leach green to yellow, and the plant, still forming fruit over my head, browns off those lower leaves as if it had never heard of them. The hollow stems of the magnificent zucchini leaves, engineered to be light and arch high as they reach out, sink down, and the leaves lose their silvery gleam.

Leaves reach a companionable beauty with flowers, but not with ripening fruit, it seems. Most of my gardening friends prefer flowers and wonder why I have vegetables amidst my flowers—though from my point of view the flowers are among the vegetables. In fact visitors fond of flowers are often drawn to vegetables like the butternut squash, to their surprise. No reasonable person has enough space for these plants, so I nick-nacked a little fence between stakes to keep them from overrunning the beans. But they just laugh at the pathos of such a barrier. Up they climb, hanging their fruit perilously, and then plump them out to great size, swelling each one toward the suave perfection of its final tan. I notice that visitors ignore the showy pink quill dahlia and move toward the outrageous squash to spy out the fruit.

One year the peppers outshone all the flowers. I had given them the sunniest spot, though I don't especially care to eat peppers. Ignoring their duty to have fruit, they leafed out instead, stem upon stem, leaves glossing their green selves all day. I read all those articles about how to discourage leaves and make your peppers set fruit, but they weren't reading the same articles. One visitor who admired them said, "But do they have peppers?" "I have no idea," I said. "They do as they please. Along about September they'll decide to have peppers probably."

Eventually, however, I bring in a couple of grocery bags of peppers. The plants are not such dandies as they appear—rather like the Spartans whom the puzzled Persian spy found preparing for battle at Thermopylae by combing and grooming their long hair. Xerxes laughed, it is said, and he won, though not by moving the Spartans. He couldn't have known that for the Greeks, virile power was indistinguishable from virile beauty when the dim human body reflects for a moment in heroic youth, the bright divine body, "the perfection of that which remains eternally accomplished in the plenitude of itself," as Jean-Pierre Vernant says. Being a barbarian, with no capacity for irony, Xerxes turned out to be no match for Herodotus, the Greek historian of the event. The Greeks, who had been unmoved by oracles of defeat from the gods before the battle, had Xerxes placed, and on a scale he wasn't aware of.

People think they are related to the earth or to "Nature" when they grow and eat their own vegetables. And they are, I suppose. But the link is not easy to understand or state, is it? It may be plenitude and perfection. It isn't work and accomplishment, however. For one thing, there's no equation there. I've been tending the tomatoes and peppers since I sowed them in March or April. At best we'll eat them for two months. In a summer of drought like this, I've spent hours of watering and bales of mulch on them. Then at the end I might lose the vine-ripened ones to woodchucks or the beans and pepper plants to deer.

Two tomato plants have inexplicably wilted. Not knowing what ails them, I have thrown good water on a perhaps lost cause to see whether I can find the cure. I need to understand how the tomatoes behave this year, which is not generalizably like any other year, since we don't eat generalized tomatoes. Every year is a beginning; nothing natural remains accomplished in its own plenitude. Each year a predator comes out in new force, as the deer did this summer, leaping the fence to feast on daylily buds and vegetables, unmoved by the illusions we rigged of a higher fence, till we gave up and reared seven feet of real wire. And while our backs were turned, the sly underground destroyers tunneled up the little annuals that please us when we look out the window from our desks: the blue ageratum and the sparkling impatiens.

"*Spes alit agricolam*," Horace says. "Hope nourishes the farmer"; the farmer, who feeds others, himself lives on hope. Irony is bracing not consoling. Nevertheless I wilted when I found my daylily buds cropped. The deer had taken away my first morning pleasure: going out to see which beauties had appeared this very morning for their only day. As I linger to gaze at their perfect freshness, opened by the light, I sense for a moment my connection to the sun.

That was gone, for this year anyway. And it's the same with every gardener—and with every human enterprise, for that matter, though those that aren't seasonal cast a stronger illusion of permanence or perfection. You read garden writers, hoping to understand the success of humans with nature, and you find they too have intractable problems. One woman describes a place she had struggled with thirty years before. Though she had moved to more congenial ground, she keeps casting her mind back to that first, sandy, dry spot, so unworkable—the "garden of ignorance," she calls it—imagining how she would work it now. Yet she was undaunted and found in her garden there the "major passion of a life."

But some complain they are so discouraged by the failures of growing things that they aren't going to "bother" with a garden again. They expected a benign response from a selected part of nature, apparently. One can't blame them. When I was a child I always resented it fiercely when I was told to count my blessings, because the advice was given for a childish, but for all that, unbearable disappointment. I know now, of course, that I couldn't have counted my blessings even if I'd wanted to. I think of the young neighbor of one of my daughters, fighting to the last the cancer that is going to kill her as surely as today's daylily will wither tomorrow. She can't keep her life, and her two little boys don't know that the months remaining of their life with their mother is a number they can count.

In these times and in this country we grow used to thinking of seasonal setbacks as disappointments. When I listen to medieval secular music, so prominently dance music, I find I cannot imagine the frame of mind of a person in the Middle Ages. In 1069 William the Norman harried the North of England in vengeance for an uprising of earls. "Between York and Durham," we are told, "he left no house standing and no human beings alive that his horsemen could search out." In the county of Durham, people had warning and escaped across the Tyne; but without any means to live, many sold themselves into slavery. So when you go to the massive Durham Cathedral, reared by the Normans within one generation of this massacre, to visit the tomb of the Venerable Bede, the historian of the Anglo-Saxons, you get a strong headache if you try to think about it at all.

Such life is more hazard than cycle. The reassuring natural wheel of return must then have been more a hope than an experience. Yet even in our hope, at sunrise we can see that the sun—which at its zenith seems simply to have arched up in the sky—is inexorably ticking off degrees we can count on our pulses. I suppose that's another sense of my link to the sun. My gardening, however, is a summer taste of my freedom. The immortal gods, I recall, do not eat, taking only the aroma of the fruits sacrificed to them. And we others, as best we can, look for plenitude outside the imperfectible body.

33 : *Out and About*

Perhaps intelligence and beauty meet in the idea of order. A garden's beauty goes beyond its flowery bits or fine specimens; we want it lovely in its "bones." Some want a long lawn leading the eye out to the beyond. Others love a bed edged with border plants defining it in the energetic, "bounding" line that Blake celebrated. In the mind, too, knowledge isn't so much facts and points of information as an understanding of the structure of things. What we really know, we know as an order.

And it's odd that order is often taken as static, a set of rules, as if life itself were not an order so dynamic that the study of it grows every hour more specialized. But dynamic orders have to be known from the inside: from some sort of beginning intuition that quickens them or from a set of master concepts that opens them into a world of study. Otherwise they are as bewildering as a strange country to a person without a sense of direction. Without it, you may find your way, of course, but you can't trust yourself to the country.

I once lived in a graduate house next door to an older woman who was doing postdoc work in mathematics. She introduced me to the idea that if mathematical formulas weren't elegant, they probably weren't right. The first time she asked to read me a paper she was working on, I laughed and told her she couldn't have picked anyone more unsuitable. But she meant it. She just wanted me to listen and tell her what I heard. This was interesting, and since all I had to do was trust myself to her intelligence, I listened with pleasure.

I heard parts in a moving continuity, a rhythm, and harmony. It was like listening to music, hearing Beethoven for the first time and in a late sonata. Or perhaps like a rehearsal, for there were lumpy bits and parts where the forward intention faltered—or so I heard. In perfect ignorance I described this to her. She listened attentively, questioned me, and went back to work.

She was a southern gentlewoman, a stranger in the North in her shyness, and a stranger in her own time and place, I fear, as a learned woman. I don't doubt that she had no one to talk with about her work and had developed a way of getting something out of the brute language of sympathy, as certain water creatures learn to breathe in the harsh air.

For me the listening was like a dream of swimming easily and strongly without any mistrust of yourself or your element: what it must be like to have a sense of direction even in a strange country—to be able to say, "It must be over there," the place you want. Those who have inner compasses are free to follow the moving order of exploration. Or, if it is the other way around, those free to explore acquire early an intuition for moving in space. True to type, as our culture goes, the men rather than the women of our family have this confidence. For them, the place where you are is not the spot you cultivate, but the center of lines radiating outward. How natural it is then that they become leaders, taking the rest of us on excursions.

And once you have the knack of getting out, there are even tracks out there. It's almost the way there that finds the place you aren't looking for. So Leonard took me for a walk on a day of gray November light when we came across a farm, hidden even though it stood at the end of a track through the woods. Past a beautiful series of rock ledges ran the track that seemed to end in a small stream. Yet we followed its traces and came to a field losing itself in juniper, and a well-built house seeming, as we peered through the windows, about as it was when someone died and left it: old furniture, a kitchen homely with old dishes and jars of canned food still on a shelf, some wood shoe lasts off in a corner. In one room a bed was made up in bedclothes now never washed, almost earthy, a temporary center for some wanderer.

Apples had been dumped near the woods; we breathed in their fragrance. I found a Golden Delicious stung by frost, singular, rich with a tang halfway to cider. The walk seemed over, but Leonard was walking away on some line of the landscape as yet unfinished, and I followed him. In another moment we were at an edge. The stream plunged to the bottom, and we looked down into a deep gorge, hanging in its own weather. He had found a deep romantic chasm, straight out of "Kubla Khan," as I might have expected.

Nearby, a switchback cart road let us down to a lower field, now in stubble. The light was a clear gray, the low, long-slanting light of November, and the field was long, long as a runway, and quiet. The ridge lines with their trees came down, curved around, stopped, and stepped back to define the space, a long plane. Unmistakably a sacred space. Strong horizontal lines stretched away. You could feel them pull, as if to pull you down. You knew if you lay prone here, your force field would align itself with the magnetic line of the field, and you would never get up again.

You got a sense of a different age, when continuity was everything, as they say it is in oral cultures, visible even in early styles of writing like the Greek *boustrophēdon*, the "ox-turning," where the words are not separated, and the writing turns at the end of each line and comes back, like an ox plowing. So writing is the traces of a track. And eminently bewildering, you would think, since the letters in one line face in one direction, and those in the next, face in the other. But perhaps it's an advantage to have two perspectives. Those persons were certainly more versatile than we. Wandering Odysseus could offer to best a man at plowing as confidently as at casting the discus. And obviously if you could plow, you had a start on reading because you could feel it in your bones.

Separated from all that, however, we braced ourselves to stand against gravity, feeling rather like disks in the swing of the curve that balances them between flying out and heading toward the center. Trees lining one edge of the field showed that the creek was there, and now we heard its sound, the same Esopus that ran behind our own land. Leonard looked well satisfied. We had completed the arc of a topography he had been tracing, apparently. I felt that I had never given Ptolemy enough credit for a system that, without explaining the movements of the planets, gave those movements an order and so told us, Bronowski says, "where we may expect to see them next."

This summer, wanting a little excursion after dinner, we hung fire between Sundown, Moon Haw Road, and Spruceton, finally choosing Spruceton because our companion had never seen it. We left our watermelon uneaten in our hurry to set out, John driving. Somehow he turned off too soon, but kept on, confident of cutting into the right road. Even small mountains are inflexible, however, and roads must follow. Before we knew it we were through Devil's Notch and out of the Catskill Forest Preserve. Still John drove on, like the son of a father who never turns back, arcing west, feeling his way through the landscape as the sun was setting. Then finally we were there, at the road to Spruceton in the valley of the West Kill.

No one seemed concerned at the lessening light by which to see the spruce beauties of Spruceton. We drove slowly to admire each porch, the old churches with two doors—one for men and one for women—the neoclassical post office, the narrow old firehouse trying to contain its wide new truck, and the beautiful valley itself, now widening, now narrowing. Along that road, one Sunday afternoon, Leonard and I had seen a very old lady in a red dress walking under a parasol. In the twice-scattered light of twilight, I half expected to see her again. Where the road ends, by the house with stone terraces, we turned around, ox-wise, bringing the man of the house to his porch window to see who was out there in the dimness.

We admired everything from the reverse perspective on the way back while the sun yet hung in the twilight parallel, that small circle of the celestial sphere eighteen degrees below the horizon. The sun seemed to cross it and twilight cease just as we arrived back at the main road. Back home we realized our little excursion had taken three hours. John, who had been hiking all afternoon, said he was going to eat his watermelon and go straight to bed. He had no trouble finding either.

I thought of what I had seen at the farm, the small wooden lasts, which suggested an old race of Americans with feet two inches wide. I found that "last" comes from an Anglo-Saxon word meaning "footprint, trace, track," and I saw these forms stepping away from me into the dark. They were a kind of carved script, traces of an intention to let your feet serve your head, to pull on your shoes and be shod and ready for your work or your walking.

34 : *Digging*

I like digging. Partly my liking is for the satisfying ploddingness of it—
turning over one deep shovelful of earth after another to put the good stuff
on the bottom and bring the sandy-rocky part up on top where mulch will
take care of it, progressing by the most simple-minded method: overlapping
your work and backing slowly and inexorably into the obdurate territory
behind you. And the freedom of digging too, when you've got every plant
out of a bed—*out*—and you see your way clear, the whole expanse empty,
like a new start, only better because you've been there before and won some
skirmishes against rock caches, tree roots, and subsoil.

Of course there's still resistance: the ground has impacted in the twenty
years this garden bed has gone its own way. As I strike my foot's high arch
against the shovel's shoulder and stoop to lift the weight of a hunk of soil,
I wonder whether my foot or my backbone will protest. But the back is in
its innocent "Who? Me?" mode, and I can probably reason with the foot
tomorrow, pointing out to it that a high arch ought to be good for something
other than inconvenience to its proprietor. With all this exercise—the bed
is forty feet long and about eight feet wide—I imagine myself developing
thick muscles over my skinny bones, but it doesn't seem to work that way.
The joints complain; so the joints must be doing the work. The articulation
of the garden depends on my own, I see.

When the bed is dug, I can at last correct its crazy pitch from upside to
downside. More hauling, wresting, heaving of dirt, more pulling and chopping of tree roots, till the bed is level as possible. And now it all looked—as
Leonard remarked with unexpected candor—at its best. From the kitchen
window we gazed at the empty stretch of it, and I imagined it as a Zen
garden of earth and earth only, worthy of having all that humus turned into
it all those years. I would rake it every morning peacefully to forestall weeds

and sprinkle it, especially at evening, to refresh us both. The garden would lie there, perfectly *inutile,* as a small protest against my own usefulness.

But the lure of planning overcame purity. Besides there were all those plants I'd got out, sitting around in various states of salvation, some of them beginning to dry. I had already been through the daylily stage, having begun all this as an attempt to save the more timid daylilies about to disappear under the stomping of the monarda and the wanderings of the phlox and shasta. I also had to divide the big survivors, and as I dug them up and found the tubers all impacted and entwined in a ball, I saw my own neglect along with their enduringness. It would take me several days to go through all fifty-one plants—for zeal has a way of expanding, and I was into my second mission in another neglected garden bed.

It took more time to separate roots than to dig them, and I refused to chop them. I bent and twisted the clumps, pulling hard even to loosen the outliers. But I didn't begrudge time spent among roots. I had never known they were so different from one cultivar of the same variety to another. As I struggled with Evelyn Claar, a particularly tenacious beauty, I got to know her better than when she was in bloom, and I scarcely needed the name tag I came across when I finally got to the center. I discovered that Painted Lady had not really let her daughters part from her and form their own sets of tubers. No wonder she had thrived in drought and bloomed with no watering. She was one, massy red root, bole and branches like an underground tree. With her I had to cut and sever, but she doesn't care, bold thing, ready to spring up stout as ever to look me right in the eye.

I was trying to keep the daylilies' identities in their names rather than their roots, however, because I'd decided that the best way of getting others to take my overplus was to sell it to benefit the library. Buyers would want information, and I amassed paper grocery bags on which I could write things like, "Late Watcher, 28 in. VL. pink w/orchid tinge." All this appealed to the latent librarian in me, though my "shelves" were two picnic tables and the hammock. I hadn't had time to get into the hammock myself this summer, so it was charming to see the pink daylilies with their silly names— So Rare, Heart Throb—swaying gently there in their grocery bags.

Their names had amused and exasperated me for years. I once almost bought a daylily named My Funny Valentine because the name started the tune and Miles's way with it going through my head. But reason held, and I thought I'd be better off simply with Miles. At the other pole, I hated it that a favorite, elegant red daylily was called Buzz Bomb. I had raised my fist and declared I would be Eve in my own garden and name the plants myself. But fine gestures pacify their proprietors, and I had let it go at that. Now, enspirited by my own enterprise, I resolved to give that plant the name of an admired friend. Uncowed by pseudo-scholarly rules, I rechristened it, marched back in revisionary energy, and changed its name on my records. The world was filled with possibilities after all. Torpor and sloth would not stand in my way. Except for that superfluous picnic table, which Leonard says is too massy and decrepit to move. So it will stay there, I suppose, till it becomes, like Gulliver's bones in Lilliput, "a monument of admiration to posterity."

All that was behind me now along with the library sale, successful to the tune of $303. As I looked for graph paper for the planning phase, I came across wonderful plans for formerly empty places. One featured camelias, another a water pool. Those charming projections had served their purpose, but this was not now the empty place of a projector in her youth, but of a digger who already possessed, dug or diggable, enough plants to fill this and several more gardens. I measured, sketched in plants, changed and rechanged my mind. Finally it was done and included three bravura passages that tied up some very old loose ends: lifting iris from their years in the storage bed, restoring border plants lost somehow in the midst of tall tendencies, and finding a beauty spot for rue got out of hand. My joints ached, but I felt pleased with myself—three beds revised and orderly. I had a little rue left over, however, including the sudden memory of a superlatively successful fellow student in graduate school on her way to Europe with three handsome fellowships whom I had asked, half jokingly, for the secret of her success. She considered the question earnestly a moment and then gave me the answer, "I never leave any loose ends."

My weeks of digging and replanting stayed with me in dreams for another week or so. It's interesting that the mind—or the dark backward of the mind—keeps working on the thing the hands have let go. Its work goes on by image making and image transforming, I see. It's almost as if I could see the images become language, with the meaning always in between, sprouting out of the images and turning tirelessly and variously into language. But not language yet; dreaming can't do that. Nightly the dreams worked toward that, and a long work it was.

The images were not pictures, though I clearly saw clumps of leaves springing out of the earth. The leaves identified themselves; I knew or could find their names. The soil was there in its wholeness. I seemed to see it distinctly and all at once, its humus, its sandy subsoil, its water and rocks, all tumbled together. The tubers, all shapes and colors were there. And the sense of my bones. No muscles—too late for those, I seemed to realize— but bones and joints as if at work, a little achingly, in tumbling up the dirt. And the sense that the images of the garden work were moving into meaning, each night becoming less "garden"—the connections, the syntax of "garden" disappearing—the elements already resonating, humming into a different order.

It's not the first time I've seen those bones at a distance, either. As I was chatting with my daughter Stella once, she lying out on her bed to read, long legs crossed, feet waggling, I realized those feet looked familiar—and the leg bones, come to think of it—and those hands I had always thought peculiarly my own. How disconcerting to see them on someone else, and in better condition too. As my daughter she has every right to them, of course. I didn't know for a moment whether I was looking at the past or the future—the future probably, for my past was never so well sinewed nor so blue-eyed. In the garden, at any rate, the future is behind me; I'm backing into it, digging at a steady pace. You can never see it anyway, and you might as well keep your eyes on the present you are turning it into.

35 : *Handy*

We want to extend the hand and our power. Tools make this easy enough, though experience suggests the difficulty of keeping in balance with our extended power. I look at my immensive crowbar, knowing that while it can probably pry out the big rocks in my garden, I cannot administer my end of it. In fact, I can hardly carry it out of the tool shed—though I don't give up doing that, trotting it down to every hopeful excavation. If only the shock of it chunking against a rock would awe inertia and tremble it into act.

Then tools easy to wield are often flawed in design or materials. Trowels especially have always a weakness in the join of handle and blade, so that I use them now frontwards, now backwards to even the force and prevent the bend that snaps the handle while I'm levering up a plant. Strong spades break the same join. The hoe I hardly ever used after I realized that hoeing was against my principles—when I used it on a mat of tree roots, it worked for a while, and then faltered on that same intenacity of joint, the failure of handle to hold.

Even the aesthetics of a tool may conflict with its usefulness. I struggled along with a leaky galvanized watering can because the green plastic replacements were hideous. When I finally found a new metal can, I lost my head and bought the five-gallon capacity, to the detriment of my shoulder bone on long hauls. So I haven't thrown away the old one, because its slow leaks are still in balance with my short hauls.

Naturally I look at pictures in catalogues of ideally sturdy and beautiful tools—most of them forged in England, where the Industrial Revolution evidently sank deeper than I ever realized. These are boldly priced, and no wonder, considering the seasoning they probably undergo in a long haul across the ocean. I've considered hinting that a beautiful spade would make a good Mother's Day gift, but it might take a consortium of relatives to buy it.

There are those who take tools seriously, as I discovered when a former neighbor desired a new kitchen. It sounded like a wonderful thing, for her husband didn't mind spending any amount of time to get the right equipment or match pieces of cherry wood. He loved wood and tools, but was hard to galvanize and didn't finish the kitchen during her tenancy of it, I believe. He kept a prized saw under the bed to prevent unauthorized borrowing—very understandable. And a motherless fawn he had rescued understood the importance of a good hiding place and slept under the bed on the saw, preferring probably not to be borrowed any further either.

But the surprise came when the lady described her new stove—electric (just when electricity had shot up in cost), but not a coil or even a glow showed on its white ceramic top, suggesting that you could cook almost by imagination. It was the most expensive stove in the county. As it turned out, she didn't care for cooking, a fact I realized when she gave me the formula from a magazine for a casserole that combined hamburger, cottage cheese, olives, and pineapple in a way that made my blood run cold. And all this while my friend Molly was testing the recipes for her magnificent second cookbook on a stove that had only two workable burners and an oven that had to be opened with a broom handle. In due course Molly got a more reasonable stove, but her conception of herself as a cook never depended on the stove.

I wondered then how many perfect studies are fitted out for those who never write the book, how much sports gear is bought by would-be athletes—how much of any undertaking has remained in the tackle or interior decorating. Maybe what we aspire to is the glimpse we get in a sleek new tool of skill itself, easy, powerful, emerging almost naturally in the beautiful thing: the line drawing, the crystal drops of Scarlatti, the fine cabinet, the corn custard, the jar of *rillettes*, where the elegance of the unencumbered person shines for a moment in the completion of the act, like the diver in the dive.

You can see the fun of perfect freedom from any connection of handle and blade in the duke's *studiolo* in Urbino. No one ever studied there or pretended to. The skill displayed is not the ones praised—learning and command—but the inlaying of beautiful woods to create the illusion of shelves, cabinets, arms hung up, a lute lying unhanded for a moment, precious books, and even a caged bird, a bit of nature apparently in tune here with the art of man. Since there's nothing actually in the room but the walls—it's all *trompe l'oeil*—the skill conceals itself in order to reveal itself the more.

At the other extreme is the monumental kitchen of the Cistercian monastery at Alcobaça, showing once and for all that there's nothing modest about simplicity. It speaks its purpose, to feed the monastery's denizens, by rule "one less than a thousand." The ceiling reaches sixty feet high, for starters, with huge windows in the clerestory shining cool light on the surfaces, all tiled in pale, bluish gray. The marble work tables look like giants' benches. The open-hearth fireplace in the center is surmounted by the glorious shaft of a hooded, tiled chimney soaring fifty-eight feet. Someone described this hearth as "vast . . . enough to roast six oxen at once," an unnecessary aggrandizement which suggests that he either had not seen the kitchen recently or had never observed oxen.

The question is moot anyway since twelfth-century Cistercians abstained from meat and would not have been caught red-handed with an ox in their kitchen. They did eat fish, however, and—never small-minded—diverted a tributary of the Alcoa River through the far end of the kitchen for water and to fill a holding tank. The always cold-running water is fresh enough to keep trout. The perfect kitchen. Standing in it, you want to clear the tourists out, stock the fish tank and start the fires, locate the flour and leavening, and begin making your loaves *ad majorem gloriam Dei*—or at least to the ordinary and apparent glory around you. You would learn then, probably, that the height of the kitchen is part of the rising of the bread.

Yet with all its enlargements, the hand itself is more remarkable than any of its tools. Maybe our submerged sense of its unique powers and complexity inspires the glorification of its implements, but the hand is far more than a tool user. Susanne Langer observes how the hand efficiently and swiftly perceives the most extensive and refined qualities: "form, location, size, weight, penetrability, mobility." It can judge surfaces, edges, and depths, "volume imbued with . . . often nameless qualities." Perhaps most striking, a hand can count. And two of them generate the algorithmic principle of the decimal system. It is on the brink of intellect, and has probably brought us there, this hand that can judge, measure, count, reach to consequences and the nameless qualities underlying experience.

Langer thinks its greatest power in our evolution is not as a tool-wielder but as a sense organ. Bountifully sensitive, discriminating, the human hand—unlike any animal hand—is aesthetic, attracted and repelled by what it feels. Experiences of aesthetic tactual values "readily take on metaphorical significance," Langer says (in one of her key ideas), and so they enter into our "most peculiar achievement, speech." It was Langer's great life work to show that articulate feeling leads to art and to mind. This marvelous hand, no wonder it flows past handle and blade, past even flame, to the good we imagine grasping.

Or the good we make. Experiences of touch enter into speech when we write and savor the elegant balance of means to end in pencil and paper. I am looking at a collection of pencils worn down to stubs by the local writer. The shortest is an inch and a half long and still has a point, a bit of eraser, and a visible number, 2. They aren't beautiful—some are crudely pared, their paint is dented and scratched, their dirt has been polished into them as they rolled around in old pockets with loose change. But they have been sufficient. Back from his run, a drop of sweat still slipping down his temple, their owner stands at his tall dresser, jotting on the back of one of the old envelopes he has folded handily everywhere about. His ideas have been running with him, and he jots them while they're limber.

The stubs are not poor shards; they've wielded the inertia of words. They became eloquent as they were spent and are now almost too human to throw away, the tools of a person who doesn't wait to study till he has a study, or to write until he has everything just right. He prefers pounding a manual typewriter to the purity of electronics, and when I ask him why, he says that writing ought to be as physical as possible since it tends so strongly to immateriality—the intenacity of thought, I suppose, the liability of the blade to slip its handle. But the intelligent hand with its pencil knows how to even the force.

Year Six

Two weeks ago snow was still piled halfway up the little house across the road, threatening to break in its windows. And now, the third week in April, it's melted even on the hills around the reservoir. Grass is fiery green from all the nitrogen in the snow. The young sun runs his course in the Ram and, ramlike, butts, pushes, thrusts everything on in surges of energy, springs everything forward like the wind pushing the water over the spillway. Two weeks ago the reservoir was just about full; today it's spilling. We watch it late in the afternoon, when the sun's rays level with the water, pour to the edge, but don't spill over.

It looks like the edge of the world, that edge I thought as a child that the world had somewhere. Somewhere after all, there had to be an end. I knew they said the world was round, but I had talked this over with other children my age. We had tin globes painted blue with little colored countries on them, so we had the picture, but we agreed that the real world couldn't be round. It didn't make sense. You would fall off. My father filled a bucket with water and swung it round and round to show me that centrifugal force kept the water from falling out, just as centripetal force—represented by the pull of his muscles—kept the bucket from flying off into space. It was an exciting demonstration, but it didn't make any difference to the fact that the world couldn't be round.

The edge of the world was like the rim of the teacup we children filled with water, running in drops slowly, watching the surface tension defeat the idea of leveling. The little water dome skinned with air—until the cup brimmed, the tension broke, and water sheeted down, clinging to the porcelain sides as it had to the underside of the air.

I wanted to see the edge of the world like that, though I don't know quite where I thought I would be standing out there. Now Leonard and I watch water pour over the 120-yard-long, curved zigzag of the reservoir's edge, down its five steps into the handmade runway sweeping the water away. The water thins out on the catch basin, glittering over the paving whose stones have been set together on edge—thousands of them set by hand. Shallow enough to catch the edge of every stone and make a wrinkle catching light, the water moves and winks. Even now at day's end, the soft light flickers across it and brightens, watering the water with a hundred thousand dashes of light.

Looking at the curve and shape of the zigzag and the design of the basin, you know the whole thing has been planned so that the overflow would be dispersed and contained even in a flood. A stone wall juts out in the catch basin like the prow of a giant ship, dividing the waters as if the Creator had been a ship builder, and sending them away downhill to form the Esopus again. The reservoir must be the last handmade monument in the Northeast; I can't imagine the labor of paving the basin. As the water winks over its well-set stones, you can feel the handmadeness of it just as you can feel hands make a Scarlatti sonata sound out of the harpsichord.

We go down to see how it all comes out at the spillway gorge a quarter of a mile away. Here the whole Esopus thrusts down through a narrow gorge—a notch really—boiling down, shooting up spray, down into the long, narrow pool where the water is always green. Then it narrows once more to go through a neck of rock. This speeds it up again, the water from one side streaking and pulled under the water from the other side, like musculature, Leonard says, or perhaps like the diatonic and chromatic rows of strings of the old Spanish *arpa doblada* crossing over each other to be available to either hand and transmitting the force of the harpist's muscles as if they were refined extensions of his tendons.

Here where water speeds and churns you can see the abstraction of water, how its action staticizes, fluidity made permanent, in one of our oldest philosophic paradoxes. It holds its leap in air. Thousands of gallons of water pour over every minute, but the pattern stays. Of a million drops, one stands in the same spot in the air as the preceding one does (whose falling you can never see) as if it were a single event, though a million drops sustain it. The pattern of the rocky gorge, its rock hollows and rock drops, casts itself in water as its reverse image, as if water were bronze, and the rock were the mold of the casting. The water seems the convex of the rock's concave, kept aloft by the permanent force of its own changing, a cosmic centrifugal balanced by gravity.

The force of all that physics is scary. Two young boys, not scared enough once during an unexpected July spillover, jumped in the long pool and were instantly dashed among the rocks and killed. We want to see force in a more human form than this. It is easy to imagine the water gorge sometimes as an impersonal shape-making power and sometimes as human fluency. But we humans are as careless and destructive as we are creative. I think of the moment when John Aubrey said he became aware of the past as a thing thinkable and even preservable. He realized that some of his schoolmates lived in abbeys confiscated and bestowed in their fathers' generation, and therefore there would be precious and beautiful old manuscripts around to study. He looked up these acquaintances only to find that the men of the families, being sportsmen, had torn out pages of manuscript and rolled them up to clean the barrels of their guns. The rector of Malmesbury stopped the bung hole of the barrel of ale he brewed with sheets of manuscript. "He sayd nothing did it so well; which me thought did grieve me then to see."

There is not one intact, substantial manuscript source of thirteenth- and fourteenth-century English polyphonic music. I suppose much of it went into the barrels of guns, their tubes sucking the music in, in a reverse of those airy pipes of recorder, organetto, and human throat issuing it forth. There are only eighteen great Greek bronzes left; a thin book will show you pictures of them all. The occupiers turned the others into cannons, a kind of meltdown of the Renaissance, which reached Greece only in the form of one of the inventions the Renaissance was proud of, gunpowder. So if you look hard at an old cannon left atop some ruined fortification in the Peloponnesos, you may imagine the bronze Aphrodite imprisoned within it, singing mournfully as the wind blows across the cannon's mouth.

You could cry, thinking of the fellows in the seventeenth or eighteenth century whom the towns paid to go around with ladders and long staves to knock out the thirteenth-century stained glass in church windows so that it could be replaced with something less idolatrous or more modern. Yet they, poor men, were doubtless trying to scrape together another job to add to their meager incomes, as poor men have always had to do. Leonard's cousin told me how many jobs his old school friend Aden Sprinkle pieced together to make a living: clover hauling, thrashing, saw mill, stave mill, and the mail route. Luckily there were no old abbey artifacts in southern Indiana to break down, only the monumental task of wresting a human life out of rocky soil.

Perhaps it's just beyond us to keep all we have made in the outpourings of human genius. Asa Gray says that the tree renews rootlets, buds and leaves, and bark every year. "No wonder, therefore, that trees may live so long. Since they annually reproduce everything that is essential to their life and growth, and since only a very small part of their bulk is alive at once, the tree survives, but nothing now living has existed long." And trees are efficient. The cambrium, the continuous creator of new cells, is one cell thick.

We are more wasteful than plants, but I guess economy on our scale is much harder to manage. Though we mourn our lost Aphrodites, a very large part of our bulk is alive at once. We have apparently always insisted on filling our teacups and reservoirs until they run over, though the water has not always been pure and the filling not always disinterested. Lucky for us in Ulster County, some local men at the end of the nineteenth century had a chance to make a living and a monument with brains and sinews.

And just as I once wanted to see the edge of the world, I've always wanted to see not just the reservoir spill over but its very first moment, to be standing out there on a clear day when that mighty surface tension breaks by the landing of a couple of loons. As they drop down and dig their heels in, running over commences. The down sides draw drops into runnels, the water sweeps out into thin sheets, and its thousands of tons creep forward to another spring.

37 : *Annual*

June is everything at once—beginning and climax. I look forward to a long summer, but it is almost the solstice, when days begin their shortening courses. While I settle in to a beginning, summery flowers rush toward completion. Everything perennial has laid its plans for summer deep by now: astilbe are intense green bushes; lilies are ready; iris are halfway through. But annuals like beans are urgent, growing twenty-four hours a day. The tomato plants are starting to roar at night and will have to be caged soon. When I mention this to Leonard, he says he is getting his chair and whip ready.

In fact my early perennials nearly escape my notice, they beat so out of the tempo of my annual state of mind. The astilbes creep into bloom for almost a month, as if flowers were too much to claim or they didn't want to be seen actually blossoming. The pink one is especially fugitive and hates to be thought to bloom at all. If my eyes are elsewhere for a few days, it will flower and get it over with. It is there to nourish its leaves and live long, not to brighten its corner for me.

But June impels the annuals forward. They have a short time to stay. And I sense the logic of growth: the quicker they be growing, the sooner they be dying. I raid my compost pile to feast them. I must work harder to improve the soil that sustains their brief enterprise. I realize as I dig that the May birdsong, which used to begin like the sun's own beams at five in the morning, is over, and I have seen phoebe and catbird on endless feeding flights to their nests.

We can't seem to get enough of growth when its green reality is all around us. Before I've planted all my new annuals, I want more and go with my friend Richard on a nursery expedition with the excuse of showing him three nurseries he doesn't know. He grins at Leonard as we leave, saying, "This is really like sending two alcoholics on a bar tour, you know." The choicest nursery is small, hidden behind hedges, worked by Mr. D., the only living man I know with muttonchops. I come here as much to admire the growth of his whiskers as of his plants. He is a bit fugitive, but I can always find him by following a hose to its end in his hand as he forever waters his annuals, which he understands better than any plantsman around here. His are always fat with bloom, bursting with green, incomparable. I stock up too much and face my usual all-at-onceness: the library fair, garden to weed, plants to put in, and a neighborly dinner party to inaugurate the season.

I'm almost out of breath with June before I start. But a festive urgency is in the air and sustains us all. The party starts on the road to our house where two walkers see two other walkers with a bottle of wine and figure they are all going to the same place. They arrive together, bringing their mirth to me, already talking in raised voices and shouts of laughter—politely intermitted a moment to hear my greeting. Then they are off, still intent on their exchanges, to the fenced garden to find the purple iris budding, to smell the white ones, and to inspect the vegetables. Deep in talk, they cluster on the sloping garden path. I watch them at a little distance, entertained by the way they incline themselves toward each other but also lean uphill, compensating delicately for the tilt of the paths downward without breaking their hold on their conversations.

Flowers, vegetables, world news—everything gets a thorough going-over. I feel as if the garden has been rectified and is surging forward in the genial moisture of their regard. I should hand them trowels and the flats of new annuals; they would open up the world's affairs as they planted marigolds. They would weed borders and politics.

But now an impulse to flock strikes them, and they are off to the bed of perennials. I can almost feel the astilbe shuddering. She may flower in shame before the clarity of their gaze. Even the rain holds off. The red nicotiana threads its way among the still-small, late summer perennials as if to say, "In delay there lies no plenty." But the astilbe finds its blessing after all: "Very beautiful leaves." Oh, Astilbe, "stay and hear; your true love's coming, / That can sing both high and low."

By and by the guests relinquish the cooling air under the mulberry tree and move into the living room to warm up. I slip into the kitchen to dish up the new beets, glistening in oil and vinegar in their amber bowl, staining their vidalia onions. There are new potatoes ready in their salad and new bread to slice. As I pull down the breadbasket hastily from the pegboard, I knock down a pan lid in a clatter that brings Mark dashing into the kitchen, either to the rescue or as a reason for being in the kitchen, for these gardeners are also cooks. He laughs me out of my impatient haste, slices the bread, and samples an end.

I ask him about the sorbets he brought over earlier in the afternoon, "Do you think they would be better after the fish and before the salad? Or after the salad and before the pie? Or last of all?" He grins. Possibilities open up plenty of time. "Well, after the fish would be nice, or maybe after the salad, or how about last of all?" As he debates the issue with himself, he lays his finger against his lips, its tip touching his nose in "the gesture of wisdom," as Leonard calls it.

At the table we pass the first bowl of beets and begin on the second. When it gets to Molly, she takes a gentle spoonful, saying, "We're all trying to restrain ourselves." Mark mops up the juices on his plate with bread in a businesslike way. At a little distance I get the best view of Lisa's beautiful straight back, her head poised like a flower listening. Guests keep busy passing dishes, when they can hear a request above their talk. They are at leisure and urgent, and so am I. The salmon is ready, but I make the sauce at the last moment, swirling butter quickly, without a second look at the sauce in case it broke on the last swirl.

New lettuce and arugula—Molly and I eat our salad with our fingers, one leaf at a time, a practice that has made my well-bred daughter shudder, though I consider it a delicate undertaking, my gesture of wisdom in the headlong impulse of early summer. One's fingers take quite naturally to good olive oil. Molly slices the two varieties of rhubarb pie she made while I did my stint at the library fair. One is a birthday pie for Leonard with a pastry cap and a strawberry bearing a toothpick banner. Finally Mark takes charge of his sorbets—lemon, and lime with a dash of ginger—handing the vodka bottle to Jim next to him to administer a capful to each serving. The finest fruits have come last, after all.

It is raining at last, though very softly. We gardeners are glad to hear it, for we've had two dry weeks, and the rainfall in June pretty much predicts our summer's share of rain. As the guests begin to leave, Lisa, who has paused in the doorway, finds herself shaking hands with them. "I feel like the hostess," she laughs, so I too move past her and shake her hand. Mark steps to her side and waves, "Good-bye now and don't worry about those dishes!" In the rain some walkers become riders, but Mark and Lisa, guests once more, refuse even an umbrella and set their feet firmly on the road, their bare young heads nonchalant as water lilies in the watery air.

Perhaps we are like the plants, birthed out of the earth into the air, changing out of them and into them. Asa Gray says that "vegetables live upon earth and air, principally upon the air." But then why am I working so hard at improving the earth if vegetables live principally upon the air? How can I improve the air? Yet I know some plants live in sand or chalk or even air. And I know that a plant burnt loses almost all of its bulk and becomes a spoonful of ashes. The burning, Gray says, "has merely undone the work of vegetation, and given back the materials to the air just in the state in which the plant took them."

Yet, I learn, the compost I give my plants creates air by its decomposing, the rich air of carbon dioxide. The roots take this in more abundantly than do the leaves. So I am, after all, improving air. And maybe myself. With the pressure of schoolwork lifted, I feel airy ideas surge forward in my head, all scorning time and wanting to be present at once. I hardly have patience to set down one word at a time. The ideas will prove mostly vegetative, but anyway, present mirth hath present laughter. I live principally upon air myself, I guess. In June your annual weeds grow as riotously as your chosen annuals, and you can hardly tell them apart. Perhaps life will laugh and bless them all (since youth's a stuff will not endure).

38 : *The Elemental Feast*

Past the middle of May, and the leaves in the country are still a light filigree of greeny-golds, yellows, or a bronze and tender rose. The spring is coming here that is over in the city. With the early morning sun at our backs, coming toward Osterhoudt's we see his great hay field shimmering, each tip of rye silver in the sun while the tops of the oaks beyond it are tufting and rounding out bronze greens like sculptured tapestry. The bliss of spring is to find it again. I was too harried to pay attention to it the first time it appeared; head down I went through the good light doing spade work. In the city now spring is way past its golden leaf, but going north we drive very simply into weeks already past, leaves getting smaller and smaller.

And the city trees came out in lesser light. As we drive the road to the country, we see May light pouring over April branches and April chilly ground. Bigger and more splendid than the light of the Ram, this is the light of Taurus, a kind of Botticellian bull in the way he loves youthful beauty in a sheer veil of a dress just scattered over with gold tendrils turning into leaves, but not a fig leaf in sight, as there probably was not in the age of gold.

The road gains altitude for half an hour and takes us further back. How impatient the people here must be: waiting for spring, their inflorescence chafing them, their sap warming, but not powerful enough to extend their branchy reach into grasp. They are probably doing all the foolish things people do in such states of mind: breaking up ground that is still half crystal, clearing good wilderness into chaos, burning their power into the night to bring spring on by morning. But our eyes are sharpened by experience. We're in no hurry, and here we can see the sugar-pure idea of spring. It's not in swarming vines nor gross leafings-out but in the elemental structure of the big trees: growth in its powerful leisure letting the shimmering birches take the first advance.

We know the large trees are as young as the birches in their way, great perennial annuals, most of what is alive in them at one time forming in one season. There's plenty of light now for them to think things over, consider the nature of leaves while leaves are still flowers, project unfurlings, networks under and above ground, the intercourses of sun, sap, and earth. At home on the ridge we see that the high lean locusts, which are always above the vulgar leaf rustlings of the other trees, are just now shooting out pointing tips of green. The mulberry is quite bare, as if the idea of leaf had never occurred to it, and the strong sun rises in naked beams on my face, warm on my eyelids and lips.

But I've been waking up well before six since March, which makes you think that a real calendar is just as bodily as light. It would be an extremely odd idea that the year begins in January if it were not for the fact that the light begins lengthening then. In other centuries, all over Europe at the same time, the year began in different months: by one reckoning at Christmas, at Easter in France, and in Florence on March twenty-fifth, the feast of the Annunciation. A bookkeeping nightmare for merchants, but from a human point of view it seems right that different folks have different calendars. In fact, we have them still, when the "real" year begins with whatever you choose to place first: the opening of the books of account or the opening of school. It's like the way you choose your life, not as one of several vistas open before you—there never was such a thing—but as the moment you most know and rejoice in openly now, the elemental feast. That's the beginning that begins you, and you can't see it printed out to some December somewhere.

When he retells the story that Er told, Socrates makes a point that the souls choose their lives in the life to come. No blind force hands them out. There are good lives, he insists, even for the last comer. It is not until you have chosen that you go to the three daughters of Necessity. So Necessity is the threefold form of choice. The first daughter, She-Who-Allots, gives you the guardian genius of the life you chose. That suggests that we ought to be on the lookout for the varieties of the guardian genius, to find one that speaks to us: the generative power spreading its wings over the loggia or the animal vigor of Taurus or, it may be, the prolific power of the snake or worm under the door stone.

There must be a good deal of thinking things out in the next stage too, as She-Who-Spins ratifies your choice. Spinning is steady, patient work.

And constant work. Women and men in some cultures always carry a spindle with them, the instrument of a necessary diligence, the small work that spins out every day. So the authoritative approval lies in the spinning. Those foolish souls who chose lives of power over others couldn't really have been looking where they were going just ahead, at three women and their spindle. They were hasty and rash. They were not supposed to choose in a moment, but choose a moment, the end of a thread. So when you come to She-Who-Turns-Not, it looks as if the thread is already irreversible, and this daughter is the recognition that completes the choice.

I start my year with the Florentines on March twenty-fifth; it's a very beginning sort of feast. I can understand why the Italian Renaissance was fascinated by the image of the Annunciation. Social historians are busy with every detail in these paintings for a look at interiors, especially what the bedroom was like, because that tells them about the individual, about intimacy, and when the concept of a private life came into existence. But aside from that, it's interesting that those young Renaissance painters, all in love with love as much as the poets and musicians were, could paint the big canvas or public space they needed to paint, on a religious theme, and still make it a picture of a beautiful young man offering a flower to a beautiful young maiden.

You'd think that in the Virgin's story there wouldn't be scope for romance for the imagination of a young painter. Theology, I suppose, dictates that in his scenes Joseph be portrayed as old as possible, almost doddering, poor thing, and usually asleep in a corner. It's touching because one knows he has a lot on his mind and big responsibilities. And in the paintings of annunciations, Mary herself is demure, with a devotional book, or perhaps a spindle. But you can feel energy surge in the powerful beings of the angels. Some show a mighty quiet, at ease even on the troubled earth. The whole landscape waits with them for an answer. Some come with an onward rush, their garments billowing like the sails of a ship, their moment imperative.

Other aspects of the paintings—the airy bird on out-stretched wings, the lily the angel bears as a standard, his fiery wings, the gold-dotted rays on which he appears to have descended—all make the angel seem the human-formed figure of the sun, an idea of energy and act. It's an image of life both bracing and calming, clearly the moment to wake up and start something new, or at least to be apt and waiting. In the seasonal moment that the paintings imagine, in March, there's plenty to do, but here in the Northeast, no rush to do it in the frosty ground. I know the angel now for the light in which to see things.

He is a messenger, and like all heralds invested splendidly to present the *puissance* of his lord. But in this story a herald is sent to a young girl. What do patriarchal cultures make of that? There's no doubt about her answer, but there's no dodging that she must be asked. If you show the scene in a bedroom or intimate space, does that minimize her choice? If you show it in a public space, a cathedral, does that co-opt it? I prefer the scene in a loggia, which is partly outdoors, but architecturally part of the house, open and sheltering, personal and public.

The painters keep all the parts of the scene: the messenger of power, the necessity of choice, and the moment of conception. It's really the elemental vision of the Neo-Platonic: logos as eros, reason longing for the difference. "I am myself, Phaedrus, a lover [*erastēs*] of these divisions and bringings-together." And the Renaissance painter can make even more than the philosopher does of the idea of conceiving by the love of the beautiful—and more of the virility of beauty.

I suppose ahead of time we always imagine that choice will be of things known, as on a menu. And choice must always range widely between the more and the less active. I think I was one of those who didn't make a claim to choose because I couldn't see ahead. I simply said yes, and I was lucky in my angel. But a yes is a promise, as all nontrivial choices are, and made out of necessity. You say to yourself something like, "I can't imagine a desirable life without this work and this person." (There is always work without a person, to be sure, but never a person without work.) I don't think Necessity ought to be portrayed as grim, as are all the representations of the three daughters. I would commission a Botticellian portrait of them as the necessity to love the good in order to live well. Not necessarily to have the good, mind you. That love of a certain good is what we, each of us, feast. And the Annunciation is the Feast of feasts, of choice itself: choosing the moment of the act we must celebrate.

Part of that feast here is the freedom this North gives me to study the light in an interval of distance before I dig. When late March brings its announcing angel, there's time, I think, to be seated in the loggia, considering the garden in a feast of reason, and choose the moment to take the end of a thread.

39 : *Garlic*

The season of garlics—they are everywhere, it seems, shooting up their stiff stalks which tip and curl around as if they were going to be French horns, each ending in an "aerial bulb," a little bunch of bulbils, with their own tiny leaves breaking out as the sheath papers and peels back. The garlic needs no flowers; each bulb segment is bursting with the genius of life. So many! I'm surprised and pleased with myself to think I sowed them when I was probably busy with serious duties. Some sowed themselves, I admit, but the straight rows are mine. All have flourished except one bulb that landed on the path and spent most of its energy driving roots through the carpeting. And that one certainly shows how ready garlics are to be their own gardeners.

But small or large, and sown the first year as a jeu d'esprit, they are now our early summer crop. We love their fresh sweetness and use them all up in summer treats: to simmer among summer squash or to garnish basil pesto spread on toasted English muffins. Little slices float in the soup, and you try not to be selfish and scoop most of them into your own bowl. Supreme are the whole cloves sautéd for a moment and sprinkled like pearly almonds among the first Romano beans, tender and incomparably sweet. Once, idling in the kitchen between dinner chores, I shelled a whole small pan full of cloves. They looked too beautiful to be mixed with anything, so I sautéd them and passed them around with a basket of nasturtium blossoms as grace before feast.

I pull a few bulbs this morning and then go on to remove yesterday's daylily flowers, clearing them away while I greet today's glories, no sun on them yet, all new from the dawn twilight. Each plant has my morning attention as every day I get to know its flowering—even as it changes and moves past its prime to be just a clump of fountaining leaves again. Meanwhile, out of its own fountain, another plant is sending stout stalks every day a little further into identity. Tending them is all pleasure. It's the easiness and plenty of the garlic and daylily I find appealing.

When I come to the iris I think I ought to tidy up their row, though I don't exactly want to. Some of the green leaves are deliquescing before my eyes, and leaf litter encourages borers. A month ago we visited them every day to find the best buds and decide which stage is more beautiful: the beginning buds with purple tips just showing or the plumper buds about to shed their sheaths. Now the iris is a garden chore, and I try to avoid chores that separate garden work from garden pleasure.

The spirit of the enterprise from my point of view is that acts of gardening are a benevolent form of idling. I have to smile when people say, as they always do, "Oh, what a lot of work the garden must be!" They look at it all and imagine that weeding must be a bore. Yet the first principle of gardening is to discover the art and pleasure of weeding—or to find ways not to do it. Some acts do look like labor: pushing wood chips uphill in the wheelbarrow, for example, or deep digging. But these jobs are enterprising and usually part of a visionary project.

I could omit heavy work or hire it done, but I don't want to miss chances to find how idea is stitched to its completion and what everything costs— what ideas cost, I mean. I want to see how plants fit their little lives to the places where they find themselves. I like the habitual mild tending that yields a dozen insignificant decisions. And it appears virtuous. "I went out at six this morning to work in the garden" is a better locution than "I went out this morning at six to idle in the garden."

The test of "not-work" is that it promotes thinking your own thoughts. A real, hard-working man like Thoreau's Canadian woodchopper disclaims ideas: "May be the man you hoe with is inclined to race; then, by gorry, your mind must be there; you think of weeds." I myself don't own a hoe. I inherited a slightly broken hoe once and considered it a year or so before I decided not to tamper with my blessedness and threw it out. Not-hoeing, you have no purpose beyond looking at the individual before you. You don't think of an end which, as it comes into view, consumes the means, an end, moreover, which has to be forethought before you can even have any means. My gardening is all means and no end.

After all, we do so much dutiful work that never shows, give up so many innocent and (admittedly) empty pleasures for the sake of a good outcome that everyone takes for granted. Just think of the universal female habit of snugly growing a child or two inside for ten lunar months. That all the world has done it never made it seem less particular to me. But most of our chores just hold lifeless things together, and briefly at that.

Last week I had to stitch up a seam in the morning before I could go out. I plied the needle in and out of my straight row closing the seam, wondering how old this garment is and why I mend it instead of throwing it out. The inescapable one-stitch-at-a-time of it. Mending has to be complete; you can't leave out a stitch. And yet I only put new thread into old warp and weft. And how came that camisole to open its seam? Surely that was reckless. I could have warned that once begun, loosening is self-generating. I noticed the small beginning of it, but hoped it wasn't really a parting of the threads. Each time I washed it, I was surprised at the progress—or regress—it was making. It hardly seemed possible it was going to go so far.

But why did I stitch the seam before I went to work? Helplessness and flawed character, I suppose. That and the final realization that it really was an opening seam and nothing would suit it but mending, short of divorce. I realized it would be up to me to close the breach, as it always is. But reality is not compelling. Only a trumped-up sense of emergency would make me mend, only missing a train and spoiling the morning, the best part of the day. So I mended the camisole with neat backstitching. I mended the silly thing, since that was the only thing that would satisfy it. I missed my train and the train depending on that one. I arrived late, but with a hidden sense of accomplishment, or perhaps a surer sense of character, that I had faced reality and set a stitch against the failures of the material world around me.

But much better the stream of idling, gazing at a new, lemony-gold shining of petals ruffled like a flourish of small trumpets, while you let go your habitual stitching of means and ends—and all the buds you can't foresee flutter by like a phantasm of small birds. The aerial bulbs of the garlic nod at me like flowers. I restore my kinship with the gent who goes running past early on the road. He looked up the other morning and politeness bade him murmur, "Good morning," though he didn't especially want to. The next time he went past, I murmured, "Good morning," as a small mischief. I knew that having tendered me one "Good morning," he thought he had done enough for our relationship. He too is alone there on the public road with the cars going past, thinking his own thoughts, the stream of them dancing free and idle through his head: images, possibilities, unsheathing themselves out of the mind's plenty.

Year Seven

The mugginess of last week began to clear last night, and this morning the light sparkles as it often does only after a storm. I want to sit in the light and trail my pen across the page. I've misplaced my reading glasses, which correct my astigmatism. But luckily I don't need them in good light, being naturally nearsighted. This is a chance to use the spectacles I found when I cleared out my mother's house. I wear them mostly to be close to something beautiful, the kind of beauty that is not made anymore, I think, in the ordinary course of things.

They look more like jewels than eyeglasses, and I thought when I first found them that they might have been purely decorative, some affectation of the time. The gold side pieces, or bows, flatten out so that someone could inscribe on that sixteenth-of-an-inch surface a pattern: running triangles with tiny horizontal lines cut within them. Where the gold bows clasp the glass, beyond delicate hinges, they become scallop shells. The bridge repeats the running triangles on a yet narrower surface. But who could see all this minute patterning? Not anybody at a personable distance from the wearer, and not the owner even when she wasn't wearing the glasses, for her un-corrected sight would not be fine enough.

The lens glass may be more beautiful than the gold fittings. It sparkles like crystal, curving along its top half, five-sided on the bottom, and faintly tinted a rose color. When I found them I didn't expect to be able to wear them, since we can't put on other people's sight. But fitting them to my eyes, I found, not the shock of someone else's reformed vision distorting my sight and hurting my eyes, but a mild correction of my own vision.

My mother and I did not always see eye to eye. She was a masterful woman, a force of nature, it seemed. Tirelessly enterprising, originating, generous, she kept in play a wide-flung net of friends of all ages. When I was very young I used to think she was conventional because she was strong on the "right way" to do things—there was a right way to iron a shirt, for example. She explained why as she showed me how to do it, and to this day I believe there is one right way of ironing a shirt. Not useful knowledge anymore, but it formed for me an early realization that the coherence of reason is convincing and can be demonstrated.

About her being conventional, however, I was wrong. I was uncomfortable being different, while she was quite unafraid to be unlike others. She was the only person in her circle who voted for Roosevelt—or even thought of doing so. She was perfectly confident that she was right. I used to hear some of my parents' friends talking about how Roosevelt was really Jewish. They seemed terribly interested in this. I couldn't understand why, though I sensed something repulsive in their talk.

I wondered about the glasses when I found them, for I had never seen them before. They were probably a twenties thing, or earlier. She saved to buy them—they must have been expensive. Then she put them aside when another fashion came in. She would never have been out of style but always au courant, with a flair that defied the dailiness of life to crush it and even suggested that a sudden outrageous stroke was not beyond her—as it was not.

I remember a time I flew to her bedside in the hospital where she had had an emergency operation. She looked so tiny and fragile in the bed that I was startled. She must have been ninety at the time. She was a volunteer in the hospital, and she had a stream of visitors, ostensibly to wish her well, but really, she said, to see how she looked now that they knew she was ninety. Her black eyes were snapping as usual—if you could read the signal. Not everyone can read signals, of course.

It seems that a doctor had come in, trailing his interns, to show them her "case." She must have sized him up as a pompous, stuffed shirt, while he (poor thing) thought she was a wrecked old lady. She listened to him lording it over his subordinates, lecturing them about her as an object, the interns all meek and respectable. Then as they were about to leave, she said, "Oh, Doctor, you're so nice! Would you let me give you a kiss?" She could look innocent. The poor doctor, how could he refuse the little old creature? But how embarrassing to be kissed by a very old woman in front of his inferiors. He had to submit, the interns grinned behind his back, and the object asserted herself as full of personal life, power, and ironic sexual play. She knew how to iron a stuffed shirt all right.

She used to give me things in a style she thought I should wear—"gypsy colors," she called it in a slightly maddening way. Long after her death, one day I decided to wear a scarlet fedora she had given me. It was awfully cold outside, and I thought the wool felt would keep my head warm on the trip to town and on the icy subway platforms. I was heading down a ramp, thinking my own thoughts, when I encountered the brightening gaze of a black gent, well into jaunty middle age, but younger than I. "Ooh, Baby, that hat!" he said. "Your place or mine?" I laughed and gave him the "You're okay" sign as we passed. Though gone in some ways, my mother obviously wasn't dead yet.

Wearing her glasses doesn't prevent my occasional glances away from my page this morning to the air, light, and color outside. I don't have to look over them to see something distant, as I do with my own glasses, which insist on correcting my vision sharply in a fussy, modern way. I'm not sure I understand astigmatism, which I experience simply as slightly fuzzy edges in poor light. The dictionary gives a precise definition, no problem with edges there. "A defect of an optical system"—that's my eyes—"as a lens or mirror, in consequence of which rays from a single point of an object fail to meet in a single focal point." "A single focal point"—already I feel that I am being examined in a very clear light.

The word "point" seems to be critical. The root of the word is *a*, "not" + *stigma*, "a spot, the prick of a pointed instrument." A point, then, fails to become a point when you try to focus it. I recognize the defect here all right. Then the point gets drawn into a line, and the lines in one direction are less distinct than lines in another direction. I have always admitted I see lines in some directions more clearly than in others, but I see now I was being charitable to myself. Science is sterner and more exact. The only demonstrable fact is that I see lines in certain directions less distinctly.

Technology can only try to correct my defects, and in small, matter-of-fact ways. Reformation is another matter and lies in another direction, helped as much, perhaps, by looking at the glasses as through them. I usually feel cheered by reading the dictionary because its great learning collected by a community of scholars is an achievement of mind and social imagination. In the dictionary you meet yourself, and your defects, released from yourself and shown as part of a large world. The dictionary and the glasses I use to read it are nice counterpoints. Very large is the dictionary; very small are the gold-fitted glasses. The geometric design inscribed on the bows and bridge is exquisite and somehow personal. Someone cut it there as a small pleasure and beauty, not seen by the world, but for the pride and finish of the work. For himself he did it, and for his own way of seeing. And it is right that what seeks to correct your sight should itself be beautiful and fine.

I'm surprised and pleased that my mother and I share the same, slightly askew vision—or that she gave me some of hers and left me, way back in a drawer, in an old snap case lined with blue velvet to protect them, these glasses, well-ground, finely clasped in gold, to help me see with my impaired sight. I wonder who will get them after me. Someone will turn up who may see more eye to eye with her than I have seen. Then in time—or rather out of time—all we descendants of these delicate spectacles will meet among the raggle-taggle gypsies to look each other over.

41 : *Rainworm*

At five I wake to hear the birdsong, and it sounds especially energetic this morning. At midnight there was thunder and some rain; now by six, thunder and a downpour. With my back against the wall under the window, I imagine I can feel as well as hear the water pounding the dry earth. My partner opens an eye to see whether I am appreciating it all. Down it comes, and I drift in the bliss of a little rain-doze with fantasies like dreams trying to put me to sleep. I see my dry rhubarb charging its chambers and springing up again in a world of water and green plants. The asparagus grow into tropical lilies; birds row through waterfalls. The suffering trees drink their fill at last and consider some prudent expansions.

Rain tapers off after breakfast; it will clear and warm. Doing my dishes, I notice on one of the rocks bordering the garden beyond the window a minute creature, very obscure, a threadlike worm three or four inches long, waving most of himself in the air in an exploratory way. He is pale, a trifle flattened at what I take to be the forward end. He doesn't look like an ordinary earthworm, and he appears so fragile I wonder whether he is as enduring as they. Though some earthworms live an average of only eighteen days, they have two genes that regulate the ability of the larvae to turn themselves into spores able to live a long time without food or water when conditions are antithetical to worm life. But I don't know what sort of creature my rainworm is, and I can't think how an ordinary person would ever discover his name.

He keeps waving about—seeking something? Earth to inhabit? A rock hole to slide into? Neither is distant, but he is not making for either. He is alone and will have to figure it all out by himself before the heat of the day strikes in an hour or two. Perhaps rain drove him out of doors to escape his flooded household. Or he is a rain thread, a cloud filament dropped in the impetuosity of the downpour, the rainy equivalent of those green inchworms always descending in June on threads let down from the sky. But they are legion in my experience, and my rainworm is unique. After all he may be a cold earth dweller, tempted out by warm June rain to explore and chart far lands, giving up wife, posterity, and companions for intellectual venturing.

In rain this whole landscape comes alive and appears as what it is: a system circulating water. Our ridge is a kind of giant, rocky sponge, always at saturation at its lower verges but oozing water all down its shaded northeast face, moss always green, any ground at its feet squishy with water and watery plants, wet years or dry years. Even in dry weather, water appears in its absence in water holes, stone beds, apertures made in stone walls, washed-away plants, all courses leading somewhere, always lower down. The water ways of the land are marked in their traces like history.

So this is normally good country for plants in the matter of water. And water is essential because plants must have it to be in act. They have water so that they may transpire it, oddly enough. Only the transpiration of water brings nutrients and water up from the roots. And only when all of the cells of the plant are distended with water are the pores of the plant open. Those pores must be open to take in carbon dioxide from the air, for green plants manufacture organic materials in the presence of light from water and carbon dioxide.

The efficiency of plants in having plenty of leaf surface, layered this way and that way to catch all the possible light, means that they also lose water from all these surfaces. So the whole system has to be working to enable any part to work. Even without scientific data, everyone feels the truth of this, and it is part of the pleasure of being in a natural world. You feel yourself as if at work, part of the whole humming of photosynthesis, water cycling, bone and blood work, assimilation and replenishment, your intelligent kidneys making some lightning calculation every moment about your own water balance.

You can see the water circulation in the land, as you can't see it inside plants, or in the plants' part of the country's water. And this is a large part. Even the sea is only marginally more efficient than plants in maintaining water. "Of all the rain falling on a densely-planted" place, one expert says, "two-thirds is promptly recirculated by plants. Only one-third drains away into the ground." So the plants around the reservoir probably hold more water than the reservoir. One acre of maple woods can transpire 3,400 gallons of water a day. This the trees can lose and still keep enough for all their work. If sun, rainfall, earth, and plants all do their work, the system remains flexible.

Paradoxically seen from the outside, from the surface, all this rocky land—even when it's forested—can appear dry. The upland woods are dry over blue stone and shale. High bush blueberries swarm out among rocks below oaks thin or tall enough to let the sun down. Even beside streams where the hemlocks are thick and black, the gloominess seems dry, probably the effect of the ratty, dead tree branches shaded out by the living ones above them. Many times I have wished a certain stretch of hemlocks by the Gladpt Klipt Kill were noble oak or beech, but they stayed gloomy, making the space gloomy. Yet they made the space.

Now they've been bought by someone who hopes to make a killing by developing lots along a beautiful rock-bedded stream, and he's begun by killing the hemlocks, stripping them all away. The shattered ground glares in the summer; the sun is hateful, bleak. The rats and owls are gone. A one-way, disordered aridity defies the water courses and the skies. The poor unwise souls who choose those lots, whether in greed or ignorance, will find themselves at the dry top of a hindered and hardened water system, no longer flexible.

In the natural course of weather, warm and cold, moist and dry do not mix but displace each other in a mutuality of opposition. I imagine my small rainworm coming to me on the weather system, perhaps created by the sun in the warm air of the equator, which spins the fastest of any part of the earth, like the rim of a wheel or the outermost whorl of a spindle. Lifted up by the incoming cool air from the north or south, he would feel the cool air beneath him lagging behind his equatorial spin, forming the trade winds going with the spin of the earth. He would sense the spindle resting on the knees of Necessity.

He would move north, my worm, all this time nothing more than a spore perhaps, still moving faster than the earth's surface not at the equator. He'll miss the horse latitudes, those regions of calm and desert where no worm can live. Falling into the westerlies going against the spin of the earth, he keeps his steadfast way, my faithful one. Dropping earthward, he is hit by cold air that slides under him, making him rise, cooling as he rises four degrees Fahrenheit for every thousand feet, the air around him condensing into a cumulus cloud. And from there he has rained down on the rock ledge beyond my window.

Perhaps he is Orpheus, singing all our myths of descent. Or perhaps in a former life he murdered someone or ravaged the earth. He might recount, if I could hear him, all he has seen and suffered on his journey of a thousand years under the earth, paying the penalty ten times over for every wrong done. He looks wise. His paleness I see now is a purified state. He has heard wise words: "Even for the last comer, if he choose with discretion, there is left in store a life with which, if he will live strenuously, he may be content and not unhappy." Soul of a day, he must be enduring Odysseus who, when it was his turn to choose, "went about for a long time looking for a life of quiet obscurity," which he found at last "lying somewhere neglected by all the rest."

Then he was given the guardian genius he had chosen by She-Who-Allots, his choice ratified by She-Who-Spins, and made irreversible by She-Who-Turns-Not. At midnight in a clap of thunder he was carried to his birth like a shooting star, to the morning and his creation by the sun in the spinning warmth of the equator. He has come both from under the earth and from heaven, and I see he is already living strenuously. So some time, when the days allotted his present life are numbered, on a day saturated with rain, when the earth like a giant plant is distended with water, all its pores open, he will transpire back into the skies of those who love wisdom.

42 : *Handwritten*

My mother once gave me seeds from her sweet pea in an envelope marked "Sweet Pea—for fence—or whatever." I didn't quite have a fence for them, but I kept them in mind because I remembered how abundant and vivid the flowers had been in her yard. I tucked them away in a drawer somewhere to wait for support, having faith in their liveliness. When I got a fence, I thought about them, but couldn't quite find them. I had other prime climbers like beans and cucumbers, so the sweet peas would have to wait anyway.

I'd find the seeds sometimes in winter, just the way you do find things, always out of sync with your plans or your needs. I thought of putting them away in some reasonable place, but it's usually a mistake, I've found, to put singular things away by method, for then you have to remember your method and can never come across them by accident. This leaves you with household arrangements you could not explain to a housekeeper. Why is the little can of three-in-one oil always at the left hand wall of the lower dish cupboard? No use trying to say—it has always been there, that's all. The books in the house are well ordered, alphabetical by genre, except for the most important books, the ones we use all the time or have to have by us at all times in case of need. These are in a special bookcase and not in "order" but in place, their own places where they have always been. Unspeakably long and outraged searches go on when one has not been replaced or has been put somewhere else, like in alphabetical order in its genre bookcase.

Early this summer I found the sweet pea seeds again, and I was glad I hadn't been so foolish as to throw them away the last time I found them in December. By now, however. . . . My mother has been dead for almost nine years, and she must have given them to me at least eight or nine years before that, for I think she didn't do much in the yard after she was ninety. The seeds might be seventeen or eighteen years old at best. I didn't add all this up when I found them. In my hand I held the envelope in her familiar handwriting, and handwriting is so vivid and alive you can't think of years. A bit of handwriting seems simply to have paused and be just about to continue.

And how arduously we had to learn to make it continuous when we were children switching from printing to writing. This is my earliest memory of exercise, of methodically practicing something arbitrary, only rationally connected with a thing you wanted to do. All we second graders were making our hands serviceable when they were already so well and keenly trained, trusty and accustomed companions. Hadn't we all when we were sixteen weeks old practiced lying on our backs and then bringing the tips of the fingers of both hands together in a thrilling experience of symmetry? Not to speak of using those hands to bring our feet to our mouths in a little toe-tasting? By twenty-eight weeks we were well into practicing our release mechanism, dropping peas, toast, cup, and dish over the side of the high chair to make sure we could let go as well as grasp. And hadn't grasping itself come first of all, when we were born? All this was intuitive or developmental, for our mothers certainly hadn't been pleased with the release practice, and we had had to cross them in that—as in so much—for our own good.

And now to train this ready hand yet further, this time by method. It was almost an insult to that quick, intelligent thing. But we were going forward into "penmanship," bent over our papers—not too far or the teacher would lift our heads up, remarking that one didn't write with the nose. Papers had to be at an exactly correct angle to the body on the square of the desk. We were grasping our pens correctly—or the teacher repositioned them—and trying not to stain our pages with our ink-stained fingers. I remember my mother, her hand over mine, helping me rotate my hand to make a rounding, extending ink tunnel neatly *on* one line and *under* another. That was to learn to write *O*'s and was the easy part.

I felt a little rebellious—or perhaps skeptical that routine and rationalized method could or would melt into the easy flow of handwriting like the teacher's, perfectly anonymous and beautiful. It was called "The Palmer Method," and I used to wonder how Palmer was related to the palm of the hand—I knew they had to be connected. I don't remember the melting into perfect penmanship. I knew my mother didn't write like that and had never done so, for I had seen a school copy book of hers with her handwriting at age ten—or whatever—not Palmeresque, and manifesting the same distinction and authority it did at age forty-five.

I knew I could never be original, determined, and clear as my mother's signature revealed her to be, so I'd better stick to the Palmer Method and come out looking pleasant and agreeable. Maybe the appearance would work backwards and beneficently. Signature was an identifying, responsible mark, made in your own hand. It stood for you the way your hand stood for you and with you always. Always your signature would stand for you and call you to testimony. And your handwriting was your signature extended and sustained. That curving flow, practiced till you could make letters really be part of each other in their words, and words all slant and round one way, spacing themselves neatly in their sentences to show that they formed one discourse—all that was for the sake of continuity, of being able to continue in yourself and meet others in writing as you did in speech. I knew it was serious, a start on being grown up.

And maybe it's this continuity that makes speech so alive, its voices going on in our heads after tongues are still, along with the other murmurings which may be all that is really present out of our past with others. My mother's handwriting, black and firm, so knowing in its own uprightness and clarity, not stooping to slant, spoke as her written words and phrases did, so like her tone of voice you could hear her speak when you read her letter. The writing was there, the seeds were there, and it was hard to grasp the interrupting years, though I was late.

But I had found them, I had a fence, and it looked to be a season of good rain. So I sowed them. In they went. I didn't have a special place for sweet peas, not having been aware before that I needed them. But once I rolled the hard little seeds around in the palm of my hand, I remembered doing that before, gathering seed from the pods of the rosy, pink, white blossoming vines foaming over the fence in the backyard. Of course I would have a fence flowering like that when I grew up. In a way I had had them all this time, had always imagined that in any well-ordered garden, sweet peas would heap themselves up a garden fence somewhere.

You do the same thing when you think about your absent friends and relations while you're drying the glass tumblers and putting a nice shine on them. You hold the glass up to the light, inspecting the rim especially—the part dishwashers often neglect—and you think of this relation or that friend. Their faces and their ways come into your mind, and you begin to write them a letter in your mind, some little bit of news only they would savor. The words form themselves clearly; almost you can see your hand writing them. You polish the glasses and complete your letter, and when you're done, you are deeply satisfied. Your glass cupboard is shining and your heart is full. Your friends and relations are always there to read and write to when you need them, there where they have always been.

It hardly seems possible that your friends aren't actually there. Old continuities are so deep, interruptions don't seem real. All the arduous work we have ever done in living shows that anyway. And intention is so much deeper than consciousness—by now, I was about to say, but wasn't it always? Otherwise how did we know to grasp before we learned to release? Occasionally your friends may feel a bit neglected when you don't write your letter, don't actually express how you've held them in hand and read them for the better part of the day. But you can't help but feel, as you fill a sparkling tumbler with deep well water when you're thirsty, that you and they are more alive than ever.

After I sowed the seeds along the garden fence, I didn't see anything for a while, and I almost forgot about the sweet peas in the hurly-burly of my early summer growing. But they came up. They sprouted after all. They didn't dare not, I suppose, directed by that firm handwriting. At first they looked like grass, so slender and anonymous that I thought they were weeds. But weeds are not so nicely spaced, so uprightly connected with each other in their straight line. They continue, very slowly sending up a few leaves faintly wedge-shaped—cuneiform, I suppose. I can read it; it says, "Sweet Pea." "Sweet Pea," I recall now was what parents sometimes called little children as an affectionate nickname. So the inscription on the envelope was probably one of my mother's little jokes—just like her to turn information into message. I hope the plants flower, but if they don't, and I can't save seeds from these very plants, I can buy seeds early next spring. I hope this may not be a mark against me when I am called to testimony. But if it is, I can say at least that I know my relation to the palm of my mother's hand.

43 : *Terrarium*

The other week Perry Cobb left me a "dish-garden." He called from his yellow truck, grinning at me and pleased with his find, "You'll see it on your porch—it's nature's garden." I found it after a moment: an old soft-drink bottle with a triangle broken out of its thick glass belly, vivid green moss foaming out of the break and creeping out through the neck. Somehow the bottle had landed in a place of filtered light, its broken side up, and so moss colonized it.

The moss is like a tiny fern. I can see its little leaves set closely upon minute stems. A green thread is sending up a red "flower," if flowering is what moss does. It looks like the terrariums that fascinated me when I was a child because they were a world, a *terr-arium*, or "earth place," with their tiny ferns, red-berried creepers, all watered and sealed, their glass bell tops miniature firmaments dividing the waters below from the air above.

Leonard says he remembers catching a glimpse of the mossy bottle as he ran up to the pipeline. But he didn't see it as a "dish-garden" because he had it submerged in the big landscape of ridges and woods, rockfalls and streams through which he likes to run. It was not perceptible as a separate possibility. And there are plenty of other castaways up there: old buckets busted out of the bottom, oil drums listing, slowly taking in earth, all sinking into the mold beneath them.

So the landscape first absorbs these things and reimages them. In the natural scene their crumble and decay appear as life, growth, and community. The bottle is buried in the "scape" of the landscape, not essentially different from a rock that shivers off its earth shelf, settles elsewhere, and begins to be a little world as soil maker, worm roof, vine trellis, and moderator of temperature. Rock or bottle sinks into another perception and we don't "see" it anymore. Its new place imagines it and webs it into a new reality.

Once the old barn across the road stood as a hold for castaways: an old bicycle, bathroom fixtures, chicken-feeding equipment. I discovered then that the flooring of the upper part was oak. Reams of thick oak planks stretched out above stairs almost too rickety for passage. A little fit of thrift shook me, and I got up there before it was too late, pried up boards, and carried them down, one at a time because they were heavy as iron. I sanded some, again with great labor, and installed them as bookshelves. I thought of hiring someone to go in there and get out the rest of the boards. I began to imagine a new room I might have, a book room at last, with real, heavy oak as flooring and shelving. I could hardly believe I was going to let the boards go, let them fall down with the barn, but I did. Of course in a way I still have my flooring and shelving, where I always had them.

Now the barn has deconstructed as barn and composed itself as complex habitat. It has lost order and energy as farm adjunct and gained energy and order as a kind of earth-coral, the way sea wrecks become reefs and colonial foundations. The woodchucks, replete in the sunken wreck, sent an expedition to our yard this summer to nest under our mulberry tree. Luna moths, those great green spirits, hatch there and come to beat against our lighted windows on June evenings. Probably the place spawns small prey for the red-tailed hawks riding the ridge updrafts and crying high over the meadow. The great old beams—chestnut I think, and laced with a thousand old, tiny worm holes from long-dead worms, beams that braced the barn's upper parts—now crown the wreck and as they decay, sift down through all the fallen layers like sediment through a dark sea.

I suppose our perception is always a configured one. The Catskill landscape is simple and grand in the mountains, complex and local in the foothills. The "mountains" are really an eroded plateau, the Appalachian Plateau, but not part of the Appalachian Range. I like to imagine the range being thrust up three hundred fifty million years ago on a scale as grand as the Andes. Behind it our plateau was being "jacked up" slowly, its horizontally stratified rock beds unbroken. As the plateau eroded, it left some hard-capped spots high—the "mountains"—formed valleys and wonderful ravines, or "cloves," as they are called hereabouts. The mountains, as you'd expect, aren't especially high. Only two are over four thousand feet, as opposed to over forty such peaks in the Adirondacks. The Adirondacks are composed of extremely old rock but are young as mountains, and they are still rising, and faster than the Alps.

If I were a hawk riding high on the thermals, I'd see a northern and a southern Catskills, separated by the valley of the Esopus Creek. Driving along the creek late one summer afternoon, Leonard and I see it as a local stream, running clear, rapidly, often shallowly over rocks. A fisherman in waders is casting downstream as we pass. We ride through the usual Catskill mixture of beautiful scene, lots of tackiness, and once-prosperous houses looking like they're not about to struggle anymore on behalf of this century. A filling station from the thirties is still standing by the road, slowly rusting its single pump. Nothing here is going to rise faster than it erodes.

We head out on the road past Devil's Tombstone, through the notch and into Tannersville, looking a lot seedier, I notice, than it did ten years ago. Then somehow we strike a road we've never been on. Nothing remarkable about the small-time, hanging-on sort of houses. We see a sign, looking homemade and extempore, hanging over the road in what seems to be an urgent manner. It announces a "steep grade" down, saying tractors with trailers ought not to go. "Use low gear," it advises the rest of us. We think nothing of it; this is not the Alps. But suddenly we are where we had no expectation of being. How had we got up so high? The road is a corniche, winding around a terrifying ravine with a mountain rising massively across from us. It's only two lanes wide and falls away into a hole at one point. I am on the open, or "drop," side of the car, I who fear edges, and I lean away from the door as if shifting my weight would keep the car from tilting over and tumbling down.

We were on the eastern edge of the Catskills, apparently. The road kept winding down and down, and at the end of it, we were out of the Catskills altogether. Out of it. Thank goodness. Away from all that crazy history where the seventeenth century is so unnervingly present, where the American Revolution is around every corner, where Washington Irving set *Rip Van Winkle* without having set foot there himself, where tanners stripped the bark from the primeval hemlocks that once covered these mountains and left the trees (and their industry) to die. I was glad to have escaped it all with my life.

And why should I think of that car gone over the road into the clove, a new car I glimpsed as we came hurtling down in low gear? Its owner, if he's still alive, will fish it out in a rescue I'm glad I won't have to witness. Or it will begin its melt into the landscape. After all, this whole place melted and flowed for a few million years down from lofty mountain ranges in New

England into the Devonian Sea and its delta. And we in the Catskills are still always flowing down from somewhere else. When I'm on my ridge, I think of myself as on top, though I have only to turn around to see land across the road rising just above me. Up there I see rocky reaches behind. On them I look up once more or across at High Point. At High Point I look at Slide, the highest of the Catskills, the very top. But on the very top I look at New England mountains from whose Devonian heights flowed the ancient sea and its vast delta, the source of the land under me.

Like everyone else, however, I'm seldom on the very top. I am high but in foothills chock full of small, discrete places, local as a luna moth in June: little cloves, narrow valleys, everywhere those horizontal rock shelvings, still eroding, that mark our plateau, and ridges with a little soil and a little garden on the top. In the foothills you are always "here," some place with its own shape or scape. Our ridge is bisected by a small waterfall and sports a smaller, knife-edged ridge, a kind of high way between Susanne Langer's empty stone cabin and the tiny Revolutionary War stone house down the road. Few walk the knife ridge. It doesn't go anywhere, just overlooks the kill feeding the waterfall when it runs as a resort of water thrushes in early September, birds of passage, local temporarily.

The elemental gesture of the country is the flowing down of all the kills, gathering air as they speed along, purifying their water by all the pullings of gravity along the way, scum slewed off to the side, the earth picked up earlier in fits of haste slapped down in quiet stretches or painted over rock beds, all by the action of wateriness—energy that lets the sediments go. The decay everywhere is thermodynamic burning, producing eventually the sweet, moist air of this earth place.

I found a glass jar big enough to hold my little dish-garden and keep it moist, but I wasn't quite sure how to care for it. If I had a pleasant window seat in my book room, I could place the glass jar on the dark red of my velvet seat cushion. Lying horizontal, jar and bottle within jar, it would resemble those bottles containing full-masted ships old New England sea captains spent their land time constructing. I can imagine within my bottle a small ship, its mast ending in a red flower, sailing on a green Devonian Sea. I think I'll find the place it came from and let it go. I've had it long enough, and it probably has a long way to go yet without me.

Theory of Descant

The unwritten pages in this book I write in are getting fewer, so every day I get closer to a picture I cut out of the newspaper. I put it in my writing book where I see it sometimes when it falls out, or I come to its place as I write and move it further ahead. I can hardly bear to look at it or think about it. Yet I couldn't throw it away.

In the picture a woman lies prone on the ground, her face turned toward her very new baby. Its eyes are closed, one arm bent up in the neonatal posture, the thumb of its other hand in its mouth. The mother is dead; the scene is Rwanda, the caption says. Kneeling beside the dead mother, another woman reaches over her to pick up the infant, who will fit almost all into her hands. Her thin arms stretch over the mother; one arm grasps the baby's arm and shoulder; the other reaches to lift and support the back. Above all, I see her intent look, her mouth just slightly drawing up in pity and resignation. That look-gesture centers the picture.

In fact, she's already lifting the baby, for you can see its shoulders are raised, its head going back. In a second she will lift the head while she supports the bottom and lower back, the whole infant brought up and pressed against her breast and shoulder. Then what will she do with it? What did she do with it? What will I do with it? There's no question of doing it "justice"—justice is hardly in sight anywhere. The gesture itself is common and deeply familiar. Anyone who has performed it once has probably done it hundreds of times. It gets into your ligaments, tendons, sleep.

And it's not that words—"mere" words, as people who don't write sometimes say—can't meet the action of the woman in the picture. Words are not "mere," though you fear your own words are. Words written are action: exact, demanding, speaking what your work and time and the chances of your life put into them, and what the language itself in its prolific ordering power will generate. You can "say" something with present smiles, tears, frowns, but only something general and temporary. Only written sentences speak for long or speak for you when you are not present.

I think of a young woman friend of mine who has been trying to write about a bad time in her life. She is brave, I think, to head into it, to start right out with the multifolded bad stuff she wants to approach and—with all respect for its savage, inflammatory, or corrupting powers—to unfold it patiently, let air and intervals into it, compose it. She has written once, twice, better the second time because then she reached for an order that accomplishes more of the "wrong" side, and so is more human. She'll write it over and over again, I suppose, till she can get other voices out of their silence and into the work, displacing each voice into its own rhythmic layer, all at work, each in itself and with the others.

Another woman—and these are just arbitrary specimens—has a wonderful comic genius: a merry heart, a wakeful intelligence, and a generous common sense. And what doesn't always go with comic powers, a tender sensibility. But as it happens, life has dealt her three or four smart blows. It's enough to survive these, finally, each time with her self intact. Yet it's not enough when you want to think and work. How does that comic genius of hers stretch out, unwarped, after it's taken in brute blows? A serious work problem. And then that other thing: brute suffering may shine a little on your own array of knives, even when you haven't used them.

I remember a poet telling of a time when his psychic paralysis had become so complete—he could hardly get out of bed—that he had to seek help and was recommended to a very good doctor, an eminent psychoanalyst. He was immensely relieved, he said, to be in competent hands, to be able to tell all the awful things back there: his bad mother in all the detail of her badness, how badly she had treated his sister, his hopeless and useless father, all of it he poured out. And when he'd finished, the doctor said, "Yes, but why didn't you work yesterday?"

That is right. And when you have set to work, and are working yesterday, you have a new puzzle when your real power to speak lags behind even yesterday. There's a poem of Marie Ponsot's which begins,

> Wherever she looked today, she looked too late.
> Everything had been a poem for years,
> . . . .
> Only the tough unsayable remains.

You keep saying everything you can say till everything has been a poem for years. But though the tough unsayable (the poem everywhere implies) is unsayable now, you keep approaching it, deviously, with hesitation, cold feet, denial, and postponement. All you can do, maybe, is keep doing what brings you closer to saying and being able to say, even if that means—it dawns on you—using up all the innocent pages of your book.

Yet all the while, if you look around, someone's work is getting us somewhere, though it takes centuries. You can hear it simply enough in music where many voices are the point—or the counterpoint. When you look back, it seems reasonable enough that polyphony, beginning around the twelfth century, should work happily at its ideas for a hundred years, until another century takes another big step. Thirteenth-century motets seem unimaginable ahead of time, glorious in the freedom of their many voices, one voice perhaps singing in Latin a hymn to the Virgin, others singing in the vernacular, perhaps a most profane love song. Different voices, different texts, different melodies, often different languages. But however much they move and oppose each other, the "tenor," a short, rhythmical unit of plainchant constantly repeated, holds them together. Circling always, never developing, it creates our sense of a work suspended in time.

And even more remarkable becomes the theory of descant with the invention of new musical notation. With music writing, the Ars Nova composers of the fourteenth century can create intricate polyphony, play all the voices, each moving now in its own rhythmic world. It's all held together by the working of the theory, "the framework of note against note counterpoint," as one scholar calls it. In a way writing is the tenor holding it all now. Sweet and subtle they wanted it, allowing only perfect intervals at first, and then the imperfect intervals for a "new warmth and sweetness."

But I am centuries away from this. I can only say my picture over, and over say it again. In the picture a woman lies on the ground. She is dead. Her infant lies on its back close beside her. It is alive, sucking its thumb. Another woman, thin, intent, kneels and reaches over the dead woman for the live infant. She is already raising it as the photographer shoots the picture. She raises its shoulders. The head begins to fall back. She lifts the child with both hands, and she will support its head and carry it away. The action is plainchant, has no ending, and I can't get to it. I put it off to the end of my book, but still I keep writing toward it every day. When the picture falls out, I put it back. The pages of my innocence thin. The picture has been there for months, years, decades.

I can't say the picture—no one on earth can—but I keep coming to it. In it a dead woman lies on the ground beside her living infant. A living woman, thin, a pack fastened on her shoulders, kneels. She is kneeling. Kneeling is the only way she can pick up the infant. Kneeling and reaching. Her knees press against the dead side of the mother. She looks at what she sees. She reaches it, grasps it, is lifting it, will lift and take it. It is an infant, a neonate, knees bent—it can't stretch out yet. Large living hands grasp it. It feels the tension of purpose, of action. Its muscles tense in response to tension in the woman's arms, fingers, palms. It lifts itself a little, springs up a little. Very little, but it is not a dead weight as she lifts it. Living weight never, no matter how heavy, is heavy as dead weight, which can't finally, really, ever be lifted at all.

I'm afraid the picture is getting thicker as I look at it, however. There's more in it than there was yesterday. Voices from the inkier pages back there are getting into it, a thing I didn't plan on. It's full of imperfect intervals; yet I don't hear sweetness. I fear I haven't notation for it. And if I can't invent the notation, I will have to invent more white pages. But I have a new writing book with a good century and a half of pages in it. I can probably put the picture about a third of the way through. The thick white pages are tight, and the picture won't start to slip out again till the white pages thin again.

ROSEMARY DEEN studied at the universities of Michigan and Chicago. Teaching and writing nonfiction and poetry have been life-long passions. She was a professor at Queens College CUNY and is poetry editor of *Commonweal.* With the poet Marie Ponsot she wrote two books for Boynton/Cook, *Beat Not the Poor Desk* and *The Common Sense,* which set forth a radical approach to the teaching of writing. The first won a national award. With the Blake scholar, Leonard Deen, she is the author of five children. She began gardening as a way of entertaining herself and them outdoors.